MANUEL DE FALLA

AND THE SPANISH MUSICAL RENAISSANCE

BY THE SAME AUTHOR:

HI-FI FOR PLEASURE

BIX BEIDERBECKE

BEETHOVEN AND HUMAN DESTINY

LIVING FORWARDS
(autobiography)

MUSIC ON RECORD
(with Peter Gammond)

ESSAYS ON JAZZ

AN ADVENTURE IN MUSIC

BRAHMS: A CRITICAL STUDY

MANUEL DE FALLA

AND THE SPANISH MUSICAL RENAISSANCE

by

BURNETT JAMES

LONDON
VICTOR GOLLANCZ LTD
1979

© 1979 David Burnett James

ISBN 0 575 02645 6

31289

EH

Printed in Great Britain by
Ebenezer Baylis and Son Ltd
The Trinity Press, Worcester and London

CONTENTS

LIST OF ILLUSTRATIONS

Following page 64

ACKNOWLEDGMENTS

My most grateful thanks are due to the following for provision of photographs, overall co-operation and general encouragement.

Señora Maria Isabella de Falla de G. de Parades, Manuel de Falla's neice and a custodian of the Falla estate.

Señor José Antonio Varela, Minister for Cultural Affairs at the Spanish Embassy in London.

Señor Angel Fernandez Conde, Head of International Relations of Radio Exterior de España in Madrid.

Also, to Ms Sheila MacCrindle, Promotions Manager of J. & W. Chester/Editions Wilhelm Hansen London Ltd, the publishers of Falla's music, for valuable suggestions.

PREFACE

IF I HAVE to put a term on the gestation period of this book, it would have to be around twenty years. But in fact it goes back farther than that. The planting of the seed in its embryonic form is almost, for me, beyond computation.

There are personal elements of course; at least one strong and possibly decisive. I was taken as a boy to Spain, on cruise liners; and I am sure I 'got the flavour' as they say, in those old days. But it was a while later when it was consolidated; then there was a still stronger, more focused personal clamping. Ever since, my emotional involvement with Spain as well as a more or less spontaneous attraction to things Spanish has been deep and abiding. As a traveller in Spain I am not on the passenger list; hardly at all since my remembered boyhood. The reasons are various and not pertinent in this time or place. In any case, too close a proximity, too full an involvement on the general rather than the particular plane, does not always help. It may cloud rather than clarify the vision. It is the germinating spark that counts: and that for me, jumped in the first place long ago; and then flashed again, so that I became 'hooked' for ever. It has not altered.

No doubt that is not specifically musical and is only germane to this book in a roundabout way. Yet to a certain extent it probably does signify, if only as a kind of *carte-de-voyage*.

The more immediately relevant reason for the writing of the book is that my publisher and I think it to be necessary since, despite the Falla centenary in 1976, no book covering both the music of Falla in detail nor—and this at the present time is probably more important, because more neglected—the national and international musical climate in which he lived and worked, as appeared. Too often in musical books, Falla, like Spain herself, is treated in isolation, not as an

integral part of the European context. This is damaging both
to Falla and to Spain. Thus, to begin with, the object is to
fill a noticeable gap in contemporary musical literature.

Persons of a studious disposition may be surprised, even
alarmed, to find no music-type examples in the pages which
follow. This is deliberate, although the decision was not taken
without deliberation. But I have long ago come to the conclusion that, except with the most simplistic analyses of the
more unimaginative examples of sonata form with their
reduction almost to *absurdum* of 'first subject' and 'second
subject' and the like, the spattering of the text with pieces of
music type is a non-starter, if not, in the centre of the argument,
a *non-sequitur*, unless the book is primarily and designedly a
technical and instructional treatise. In a more general book
such as this I am convinced that score references are not only
preferable but considerably more logical. This is particularly
true of a composer like Falla, for two reasons: first, his music
is so written that only by reproducing a page of full score (and
not always then) rather than a scrap of thematic or harmonic
matter taken out with a scalpel, can much sense be made of it.
This, of course, is true of everyone whose textures are part of
the fundamental aesthetic of composition; and that means
virtually all modern composers. Second, with the greatly
enlarged availability of study and miniature scores, and their
corollary the LP record, the score references take on a further
relevance and an increased usefulness. In the case of Falla,
miniature scores are readily available of all his compositions
with the exception of *Atlántida*, and piano reductions or vocal
scores from his publisher (Chester/Hansen) for the more
nimble fingered. If a reader cannot read music, music-type
examples remain useless, at worst a puzzling check to fluent
reading; if he or she can read music, the score will be either an
already possessed adjunct to enjoyment, or will be procured.
Either way, the score reference is much to be preferred.

Those who object to political matter intruding into books
on music have my sympathy. Unfortunately, it is not quite as
simple as that. Constant Lambert once asserted that for every
musical reason why a composer writes as he does, there are
at least ten social reasons. Maybe that is an exaggeration

(though not too much of one); and in any case the 'social' includes and embraces at all levels the political. This has become more true as we have dug deeper into the twentieth century and politics have taken on an increasingly prominent, and, some would say, presumptuous role. And nowhere is this more true than in Spain since the First World War, with first the establishing of the Republic, then the Civil War, then the Franco era and finally the re-establishment of the monarchy. To suppose that any significant Spanish activity, in the arts or elsewhere, can be discussed in isolation from those momentous events is to condemn that activity to the peripheral and the inconsequential. Spanish music, art and literature detached from Spanish social and political history is not so much *Hamlet* without the Prince, as the Prince without Denmark.

I have kept it to a minimum, but it cannot be left out altogether. If what I have said offends any too touchy sensibilities, either side of the thin line, I am sorry, but I cannot help it. I speak, or try to speak, from the point of view of Spain herself and of her most distinguished composer. I am content to leave it at that.

BJ

Kingston-upon-Thames
1978

MANUEL DE FALLA

I

THE SPANISH HERITAGE

'EVERYTHING', WROTE Teilhard de Chardin, 'is the sum of the past and nothing is comprehensible except through its history.' That is true of all developments in the arts, and it is particularly true where those developments are rooted in specific nations and particular national characteristics. In the case of Spain it has unusual relevance, for reasons deeply embedded in Spanish history and in the underlying realities of the Spanish spirit and temperament. Throughout most of her history Spain has felt herself isolated from the rest of Europe, both geographically and emotionally. The physical barrier is not only the Pyrenees—a 'barrier' as much psychological as physical—but the proximity of southern Spain to North Africa, again by no means only geographical in its long-term effects. The emotional isolation, more subtle, less directly definable, derives in large measure from the Moorish occupation which lasted for more than seven centuries. The Moors were finally driven out by the reconquest of Granada in 1492; but that did not by any means end the Moorish business: it lingered on for another century in physical actuality and more or less permanently by implication.

The treaty made by Ferdinand and Isabella after the conquest of the Kingdom of Granada, itself only a partial victory, was almost unbelievably weak. It left the Moorish nation on southern Spanish soil more or less intact and effectively prevented the establishment of national unity under the 'Catholic Kings'. This had far-reaching results. Another century at least was needed for the Moorish hegemony to be reduced, and that played a leading part in sharpening the Spanish consciousness of its role of defender of Christian civilization against the infidel. And it was precisely this role that had the determining impact on the Spaniard's relationship with the rest of Europe: it made him feel both isolated and an essential outpost of the true faith and the civilized values. The idea, long held and often promoted, among the Anglo-Saxons in particular that the best in Spanish civilization is Moorish in origin is a clear example of blinkered but popular prejudice and inept propaganda. Christian Spain has always been a part of Europe and European civilization: the true essence of Spain is European, historically and contemporaneously, and is only comprehensible from the European standpoint.

Yet the picture is more complicated than it appears, and the complication arises from the African connection, as it may be called. Spain is not only Europe's most direct link with Africa; but the pattern of Spanish history is largely reflected through that link. It has been said that a Spaniard resembles the child of a European father and an African mother; and certainly there is in the Spanish nature and temperament a blending of the European and the African unique among the peoples of the West. Inevitably this admixture was strongly reinforced, even if it was not created, by the long years of Moorish occupation. Nor does it refer only to the people of the south, of Andalucía: it is widely accepted that the Basques with their highly individual customs and language are descended from Berber stock which infiltrated the aboriginal pre-historic Pyrenean race. But it still has to be repeated: Spain and the Spaniards are essentially and irreversibly European and only find their true nature and destiny within the European context.

Of course, Spanish history did not begin with the Moorish occupation, any more than it ended in the larger sense with the decline in national fortunes and prestige which began after the death of Philip II. There was Roman and Visigoth Spain, certainly not to be ignored in any assessment of the national history and consciousness. All the same, the impact and legacy of the occupation, of the plain fact of Muslim Spain, was decisive in forming the subsequent history of Spain and the Spanish character and its sense of destiny.

It also, inevitably and inescapably, had a major bearing on the evolution of Spanish art and its forms. Literature and drama, painting and architecture, all forms of music, art or popular, bear eloquent witness to the Moorish influence. If that influence was primarily in the areas of detail and ornament with the deeper influences and indigenous currents, that merely confirms the truth that Spain and Spanish history can only be understood against the European backcloth. This was as true of the mediaeval period as of the period of Spain's international greatness during the 'Golden Century' under Charles V and Philip II.

Nor is it in any sense true that the Moors and other alien settlers brought and left to a largely coarse and barbarous people some semblance of refinement and sensitivity. This is total nonsense, yet it remains an idea still coddled in the darker recesses of decadent romanticism. But any objective view of Spanish history insists that the real truth was nearer the opposite. There is evidence that many of the evil traits for which the *conquistadors* have been condemned by history were influenced by Moorish mores. A book on music is not the place to go into the finer details of this; but the fact has to be stated, insisted on, in order to adjust the historical focus and put the fundamental Spanish character and temperament, revealed as it always is and must be through the arts and as it unquestionably is in Spanish music, into proper perspective.

Although many in Spain were prepared to welcome the Moorish invader; although large numbers of Spaniards became Muslims; although the arts and customs of the Moors infused virtually the whole of Spanish life and in certain ways enriched it, the primary fact of life for the Spaniard became the guardian-ship of Christian civilization. National unification was always a difficult task for Spain, partly due to the heterogeneous nature of the population, partly because of the inborn indi-vidualism of Spaniards, both of which have continued to operate up to the present day. But spiritual unity against the infidel became an essential motivation of the Spanish character: it was the principal cause of that intense pride and passion for which Spain and the Spaniards are renowned the world over. And as emnity towards Spain in her great days of imperial splendour grew, so the sense of isolation and misunderstanding of the role of guardianship increased. Thus, although Spain and Spanish history can only be understood within the European context, internal as well as external, pressures built up to convince the Spaniards that they were increasingly apart from the central objects of their guardianship, in the same way fighting troops from the front line tend to feel isolated from those at home in whose service they are risking life and limb. And Spaniards being Spaniards, the greater the resistance to their conception of themselves, the stronger their own pride and conviction grew. Christian Spain has always preserved a high regard for itself; and as corollary the Spaniard, whether Christian or not, has become so steeped in that spiritual and intellectual background that it has long since become ineradicable. Again, this is to short circuit, probably beyond the bounds of what is normally and historically realistic; yet in a book on music the main broad lines need to be indicated only when dealing with a specific national output, and this will serve to point a necessary direction, to define a particular area of reference.

Inevitably, much of the history of Spanish music is preserved by the Church and the religious foundations. This may not make it in any sense unique; yet because of the broader current of Spain's history it does give a specifically musical variety a particular twist. Everywhere in Europe the Church was the preserver of music and the arts, especially in times of political and social turmoil and when the threat of darkness was over the land. In Spain the role of the Church and the religious Orders was not so much different from that in other Christian countries as originating in another context—the context, that is, of alien occupation over a long and decisive period. And Spanish music itself, like all Spanish art, was inevitably infused with African and Arabic influences at various levels. Allied to the innate character of Spanish music as a true reflection of the innermost Spanish character and spiritual assumption was the sensuality and charm of the Moorish culture which impinged so long and so directly upon it. And this, of course, applies not only to secular music but to the music of the liturgy itself.

It is by no means in sacred music alone that the nature of the essential Spanish art forms is revealed, despite the pre-dominance of the Roman Catholic Church in all the nation's affairs through most of its history. No less is that character and that temperament—or temperaments, for there is no one

Spanish idea or life-view—revealed and given the most potent expression in the great variety of Spanish folk song and dance. The vigorous individuality, the dark sense of drama, the emotional fervour, the unquenchable spirit of independence, the innate pride and passion of Spain and the Spanish people is all there, even more vividly and variously delineated, in the popular culture of a nation and race that treasured and preserved that heritage at least as long as any other in Europe and longer than most.

Although too great an intrusion of popular elements into sacred and liturgical music has always been resisted by the Church authorities everywhere, the strength of the Spanish variety inevitably made the fusions and transfusions direct and far reaching. Sometimes it is open and overt: there is from Andalucía a 'Flamenco Mass' regularly performed. It may not be great or important music; but it exists and is a genuine expression of the religious feelings of the gypsies of the warm south. Nor does it end there: other regions too have their particular forms of music for worship based upon local folk idioms. It is all, in fact, simply another example of the adage that every man prays in his own language and in his own manner.

Yet it is not only, or even primarily, sacred and liturgical music which is frequently infused with the letter as well as the spirit of Spanish folk song and dance and the total popular culture it represents: it is the whole of Spanish music, in one sense or form or another. This is particularly true of the Spanish 'renaissance' in music that came with the late nineteenth century and extended deep into the twentieth. The Spanish 'renaissance' was, like its English equivalent, a notable manifestation of the 'second generation' of romantic nationalism in music: in both cases, as in certain others, the impetus came from the twin and complementary forces of folk music and a rediscovery of the music of the national past.

The force of the folk music involvement was, in general, the decisive one from the nationalistic viewpoint. Yet the major composers in every case, Falla in Spain, Vaughan Williams in England, Bartók in Hungary, Janáček in Moravia, though deeply aware of the folk inheritance, seldom used actual folk material in their compositions. An exception in one way is Sibelius whose basic material owed little to Finnish folk song and dance even though his initial impetus came from his country's folk poetry and legend. But with Falla, Vaughan Williams, Bartók, despite intense devotion to the national folk heritage, the material itself is only derived from folk song in the broadest and least obvious sense: it is an informing spirit rather than an immediate source; an idiom of speech rather than a precise syntax and vocabulary copied direct from nature. Falla himself believed that folk music is best cultivated by the educated musician who does not use it directly but transforms its spirit into something original and independent; when, that is, his creative force is liberated by a profound sense of the national identity as expressed in the popular heritage. One of the very few instances in Falla of the incorporation of a genuine folk song into a major work is the quotation of the old Castilian song 'De los Alamos, Madre' in the harpsichord concerto. There are a few passing references elsewhere, in *The Three Cornered Hat* and *El Retablo*; otherwise Falla's thematic material is original and when it sounds to the contrary it is because of his total assimilation of the essence of Spanish popular music as a whole. Vaughan Williams hardly ever used folk-song themes in works not deliberately issued as arrangements or transcriptions, and Bartók moved farther away from Hungarian and Magyar material the older he grew. Brahms once said that whenever he was stuck for a melody he thought of a German folk song. The remark is illuminating; but it is also a little specious, because even though Brahms did immerse himself in German folk song he had also the entire tradition of Austro-German art music behind him and was in no way concerned to found or propagate a national school of music. Even so, it throws light into certain areas of the creative process in the late romantic period.

The very strength and distinctiveness of Spanish folk music, however, was a danger for less powerfully talented composers. Its striking turns of melody and rhythm, its picturesque qualities with their superficial appeal to non-Spaniards made it all too easy to draw upon it for surface effects and glib colouration. Much Spanish national music is too obviously of the picture-postcard variety precisely because of the nature of the folk music from which it is too enthusiastically derived; and it is not difficult to see that the weakness of much of the work of even such gifted composers as Albéniz and Granados is in one respect at least a direct result of a too facile reliance on the outer characteristics of the national song and dance.

In one respect, though, the Spanish national composer had an advantage over his English counterpart. Well into the present century Spanish folk song and dance remained an active and living reality. Even today, when it is a tourist attraction or a stylized concert artifice, it is still more than a distant memory in many parts of the country. Despite the impact of twentieth-century anonymity and standardization, folk music in Spain remains a vital force, even though it too is in inevitable decline and almost in need of artificial preservation. But in England folk song was virtually a period piece, if not a 'tea shoppe' anachronism, by the time the English musical renaissance and its consequential folk revival had gathered momentum. Already in the late Victorian age gathering and editing folk songs had become something of an antiquarian activity that for the most part constituted refining and bowdlerizing that robust idiom of popular rural song into pretty drawing-room ballads. When a subsequent generation reversed that process and insisted on collecting and publishing the original material, they still did so as though it were a living tradition instead of already a part of social history, much as composers of the later nineteenth century continued to resort to traditional sonata form although it and what it stood for had been dead a hundred years.

The reasons in both cases were purely historical. English society was violently transformed from a predominantly rural and agricultural community into a predominantly urban and industrial one in the course of a generation or so, long before there was any thought of a musical 'renaissance'. Therefore, folk song and dance, which is primarily rural in origin, had already ceased to be a significant expression of the life and character of the majority of the people. As musical inspiration it could still be, and was, a genuine source-motive. But since its social universal context had largely disappeared, there was an inevitable sense of archaism about its too indulgent use. And although there grew up a body of urban folk song reflecting the life and outlook of the new industrial population, it was never 'folk song' in the old sense and was seldom drawn upon by composers.

In Spain, however, there was no such cleavage: when industrialization did come much later, it was slow and not disruptive. Spain remained largely agrarian until well into the present century, and so her folk culture and popular music retained roots deep in the national life and psyche long after its counterparts elsewhere had faded into specialist 'enthusiasms'. Though the pace of change has quickened in Spain, as it has in all countries slow to enter the field of total industrialization, it had not at the time of the musical renaissance done much more than curl the edges of the national consciousness. The style of declamation Falla employed for the part of the Boy in *El retablo de Maese Pedro* was authentically that of the street story-tellers who were still to be heard in Madrid and the big cities during Falla's lifetime and may still be heard in the outlying districts today. But you will not see today a Morris dancer in England, on village green or manorial lawn, or hear a country folk singer who is not old and resurrecting it from memory (nor would you have done 50 years ago), unless it is a put-on show, a deliberately perpetrated anachronism. And that is the difference: it was more important then, when the national music revivals were playing their early hands than it is now. Now the perspectives are a lot clearer.

The relationship between agriculture and industry was generally important in the search for the musical renaissance. Whether the nationalist obsession and the cult of an ancient folk-song inheritance is evidence of a musical inferiority complex is perhaps debatable. What is not, is that the impetus always comes from a rural past, never from an industrial present, even when the industrial present is, nationally, what matters. But it still makes a difference if the rural past and pastoral dream is a continuing social reality instead of an anachronism.

Despite the divergences in the social and industrial evolution of the two countries, the history of Spanish music shows an overall correspondence with that of English music. There is the same adventurous creativity in the early stages, rising to a peak in the sixteenth century, the golden age of vocal polyphony, with the Spaniard, Victoria, and the Englishman, William Byrd, sharing honours with the Italian, Palestrina, and the Flemish Roland de Lassus in a period of great and varied activity. Then there is a parallel decline with foreign domination—in Spain that of Italy, in England that of Germany —overwhelming and more or less stifling the native genius well into the nineteenth century. Subsequently, the native tongue began to stir, the late Romantic urge became infective, and a major resurgence was initiated, in the first place by scholars, teachers, idealists, then consolidated by the emerging composers around the turn of the century. And in Spain, as in England, before a national renaissance could be instigated, it was first necessary to go back into history, to rediscover and redefine the roots, to explore the all but forgotten glories of the musical past on the one hand, and the latent potentialities of folk song on the other.

In the latter respect, Falla and the Spanish nationalists had more in common with Vaughan Williams in England and Bartók in Hungary, than with someone like Edward Elgar, the first progenitor of an English renaissance in fact rather than theory. Elgar had little interest in or affinity with folk song: his historical sense was emotional and literary rather than purely musical. In one sense, this made him a more truly and profoundly national composer than any of the English folk school except Vaughan Williams at his very best, for only he bridged the yawning gulf that lies in wait for any artist who sets out upon a deliberately nationalist standpoint. And that gulf is precisely the one between folk art and national art; the first domestic and limited, the latter ranging forward and outward. Falla, who had the kind of instinctive affinity with folk song and dance virtually inevitable for any Spanish musician bridged the gulf in a different way—and in the end perhaps more completely than either Elgar or Vaughan Williams, though on a considerably smaller scale. The scale might have been altered and greatly expanded had the large choral/ orchestral work on which he was working over the last twenty years of his life achieved what it was intended to achieve, for it was precisely that problem to which Falla addressed himself and hoped to solve once and for all with *Atlántida*. But he never finished it, so the question remains forever unanswered. In this matter, though, and within this specific focus on a comparatively narrow range, scale is not paramount.

The musical histories of the two countries, Spain and England, thus ran on broadly parallel lines. The most immediate difference—apart from the sociological position of the respective folk idioms and cultures—is that Spain lacked the solitary indigenous genius in the seventeenth century that England produced in the short-lived figure of Henry Purcell. The later English composers, notably Michael Tippett and Benjamin Britten, found much inspiration in Purcell; but the Spaniards had no such point of intermediate reference, as we may call it. Scarlatti, who was to become such a point of reference, was a different matter, being Italian and not Spanish, even though he substantially hispanicized himself in his later life. Yet Purcell was an isolated figure, one who by personal genius shed a passing light on and into an otherwise uninspiring age, but whose rare gift was far more hampered than stimulated by the surrounding mediocrity. His undoubted genius for drama and music must have made him a major operatic composer if he had not been continually hamstrung by the prevailing taste which imposed on him libretti of astonishing banality.

Nor was the foreign domination during the 'middle period' in either case general and indeterminate only. It was more positive than that. In Spain, Domenico Scarlatti, and in England first Handel then Mendelssohn and Brahms (though Brahms in fact never visited England, despite temptations and invitations) gave the process a personal and individual turn. Scarlatti lived for much of his life in Madrid; and though his music shows unmistakable influences of the Spanish environment in which he lived and worked, he remained at heart an Italian and exerted as profound an influence on Spanish music as it did on him.

But it was in the field of opera, where Scarlatti had also been active in his younger days, that the Italian domination of

Spanish music was most decisive. Even the *zarzuelas*, the popular operettas of Spain, which might be expected to be uncompromisingly if not always obviously Spanish, are often only superficially so. The underlying musical style, especially during the later nineteenth century, is often basically Italian; and some of the well-known *zarzuelas* are little more than watered down Italians. Indeed, most Spanish music for the lyric theatre during the eighteenth and nineteenth centuries is hardly more than second-hand Bellini, Donizetti or Rossini with a smattering of Puccini coming in during the later stages. The colour and vivacity of Verdi is almost entirely missing except where the true Spanish voice breaks through and the national energy is unleashed, as it is in the true classic *zarzuelas*. Falla himself was keenly aware of this and dedicated his life to the exorcizing of it. If he thus tended to undervalue the Italian opera composers, it was as much because of their debilitating influence on the whole of Spanish music as on account of a clash of temperament and artistic ideals.

But the domination remained; and it was a major element in the background against which the renaissance of Spanish music had to take place.

The extra-musical reasons for the decline of both Spanish and English music at a time when the art of music generally was on the upsurge elsewhere in Europe, appear to have been opposite if not complementary. In the case of Spain it coincided with an overall national decline from world-power status; in England it equally coincided with the economic rise consequent upon the Industrial Revolution and a corresponding political rise in international power and prestige. Precisely how much these particular forces can be related to the musical decline is hard to say, but they were clearly operative. If, in Spain, the general falling away from the old glories seriously deflated her position in the imperial world, it certainly did not diminish the Spaniard's idea of himself as a special and superior person, so that the musical deficiency can hardly be held to have been the result of a lowering of vitality or a national inferiority complex. In England, on the other hand, the sense of growing superiority seems to have coincided with the increase in imperial and industrial power. Nor would it be tenable to argue that the decline of English music was in any meaningful sense a direct result of that power and prestige and the specific feelings associated with it. It is true that English philistinism and the concentration on material prosperity was staunchly reinforced by the rise in national fortunes; yet English literature of the period is by no means wanting in comparison with what had gone before and what came after. Personal taste may argue the case for an earlier or a later literature; but in music, and despite some valuable work of restitution in our own time, there is no real case to argue.

Yet it is perhaps not sheer coincidence that the musical histories of Spain and England run on broadly similar lines: there may well be some deeper running strand of synchronicity. The partial isolation of both from the mainstream of Europe, though for different reasons, no doubt had a good deal to do with it.

To follow through that similarity is not simply to harp upon a private conceit. It is worth urging because it helps to illuminate from several angles each of those national developments, declines, and subsequent rebirths. And this is the more significant because here we have two major nations which once had a musical glory, lost it, then by singular effort regained it in a manner not quite repeated elsewhere. For Italy, France, Germany, each with a long and continuous musical tradition, the nationalist movements in the nineteenth century which came in the wake of the Romantic crisis did not and could not have the same meaning. There was no question of a revival or 'renaissance': there was no need for it; a change of emphasis was all that was required. And smaller nations, Norway, Hungary, Finland and others which found new and individual voices through musical nationalism, and usually had at least one major composer to define and confirm them, either had no strong tradition to lose or had kept to a purely folk and local one. Russia, as always, stands to some extent apart, constitutes an eternal exception, for reasons too complex and insufficiently relevant for a book of this nature. Only Spain and England follow out the exact parallels that significantly illuminate each other from this immediate viewpoint.

In fact the similarities do not really begin to operate much before the fifteenth century, and they only become strongly etched in the sixteenth. Spanish musical history is longer than English, running back as it does through the seven centuries of Arabic occupation and the consequent intermingling of disparate cultures. The Mozarabic Rite, adding a striking variant to the standard Georgian rites and enduring in Murcia until 1266, was only one example. A number of collections of songbooks and codices preserve the Spanish heritage from the Middle Ages to the Renaissance, notably the 'Cancionero Musical de Palacio', the 'Cancionero de Upsala o del Duque de Calibria', the 'Cantigas de Santa Maria', the 'Codex de las Huegas' and others. There is also the 'Codex Calixtinus' which outlines the musical activities at Santiago de Compostela, that centre of Christendom during the time of the occupation, where the tomb of St James the Apostle became from the ninth century on a shrine almost as important for Christians from all over Europe as that of Jerusalem and the Kaaba in Mecca for Muslims. Santiago, though itself sacked in 997, was the centre of the only part of Spain not occupied by the Moors, and as well as being a bastion of the Christian faith was also a major centre of music where a small school of composition flourished at the monastery. The 'Codex Calixtinus' is generally regarded as one of the outstanding documents in the history of the music of the Middle Ages; but all these collections, plus many more, are of the first importance.

For the progenitors and moving spirits of the Spanish musical renaissance at the end of the nineteenth century and the beginning of the twentieth, the preservation and rediscovery of these collections was vital. Felipe Pedrell, often called the 'father', sometimes the 'Moses' or even the 'Don Quixote' of the Spanish revival was a great and passionate lover of the old music as well as of the popular type in which he saw salvation for the national art. Falla himself was no less a devotee, especially of the old courtly music and the Romanesque music of the Middle Ages, both of which combine with a sharply modern astringent style owing something to Stravinsky in places in a way that makes *El retablo* perhaps the most completely and satisfyingly Spanish of all musical compositions.

Pedrell, who was born in Tortosa in 1841 and died in

Barcelona in 1922, was the most erudite musician of his time in Spain; but he was largely self-taught. As a choir boy in Tortosa he acquired a close knowledge and practical experience of Spanish church music. It was Juan Antonio Nin y Serra, with whom he appears to have studied for a short time, who urged him to base his musical exercises on songs sung by his mother. One of Pedrell's most important achievements was his publication of a complete edition of the works of Victoria, including some valuable research into the great composer's life and the revealing of a number of hitherto unknown or un-recognized biographical details. Another was his edition of a collection of the compositions by a number of the leading Spanish composers of the sixteenth and seventeenth centuries, including Victoria, Morales and Cabezón, under the general title of *Hispaniae scholae musica sacra*. At the other end of the musical spectrum his published collections of Spanish folk music (*Cancionero musical popular español*) were of immense importance, even if the 'purity' of his editions was occasionally suspect. In between, musically, came his editions of Spanish theatre music and organ works. He was, especially in his advancing age, reported to have been a difficult and disillu-sioned man. He was seen as a great scholar and teacher but his own compositions, which were numerous and encompassed a number of operas, found no public favour, and posterity has largely confirmed the contemporary verdict. On the other hand, nothing can detract from the importance and influence of his pioneering work, even if it was only recognized by a select few among his colleagues and juniors. Falla was by no means the least of these.

But it was during the so-called 'Golden Century' and in the approaches to it that Spanish art in general and Spanish music in particular rose to its greatest heights. The gradual unification of the nation following the marriage of Aragon and Castile with Ferdinand and Isabella and its rise to world power under Charles V and Philip II, the period which saw the final conquest of the Moors; the voyages of Christopher Columbus which, though like himself of Portuguese origin, still formed an important part of the Hispanic world's growth; the conquests in South America and the spread of Spanish power into Italy and the Netherlands; saw also the peak of Spanish art in most of its various forms.

In music this supremacy was focused most clearly in the person of the greatest Spanish composer of the period, Tomás Luis Victoria. Victoria, who was born in 1548 and died in 1611, lived much of his life in Rome and his name has sometimes been Italianized as 'Vittoria'. But there was nothing Italian about Victoria except residence; he was a Spaniard through and through. He composed nothing but liturgical music in an age when secular and instrumental composition were growing in influence and importance. Yet he was by no means a musical diehard or reactionary. His Spanish predecessor, Cristóbal Morales, who lived from around 1500 to 1553, was a true conservative, though certainly a musician of genius. But Victoria was altogether of his time and period, and in some ways in advance of it as a composer. His polychoral compositions, using two or three choirs with great power and imagination, are decidedly forward-looking; and his use of written-out organ parts makes them seem, in context, even more so. His dark sense of drama, often sombre and searing, reminds us of the paintings of El Greco, while his profound mysticism, reinforced by his association with St Philip Neri, and possibly with St Teresa also, has that particularly Spanish quality of spiritual passion. Indeed, Victoria was a man and composer who exemplified in himself the leading characteristics of the typical Spaniard of his time. His devout Catholicism was as profound, if not as fanatical, as that of Philip II; his Jesuit sympathies were in line with contemporary Spain's fight against the Lutheran heresy as well as against the more general enemies of the nation; while his dramatic fervour was specifically Spanish in its fire and intensity, as well as in its concomitant pride in national identity, a product of his Castilian ancestry. Victoria in music was one of the artistic peaks of Spain's renaissance, as Velasquez was in painting and Cervantes in literature.

Although the tradition of Spanish music was still, under the influence of the Catholic Kings, los Reyes Católicos, predominantly liturgical, there was also important work being done in the secular and instrumental fields. The blind organist

Antonio de Cabezón was one of the leading instrumental composers of the period, and it is likely that he exercised a direct influence over English composers when he accompanied Philip II on his journey to England to marry Mary Tudor. Then there was the school of Spanish *vihuelistas* led by Luis Milán but including also such admirable figures as Luis de Narvaez, Alonso de Mudarra, Miguel de Fuenllana, Enriquez de Valderabano, Venegas de Henestrosa in a more general way, and finally Esteban Daza who published the last work devoted solely to the *vihuela* before it was superseded by the guitar. The Spaniards were the first to take the lute over from the Moors and in fact the lute and the *vihuela* co-existed in the courts and noble households. But the general move in Spain during the sixteenth century was strongly towards the flat backed and 'crushed' bodied *vihuela,* which in its turn evolved into the five stringed *guitara española.* Thus the music for *vihuela* was not the Spanish variety of that for the lute and the *vihuelistas* were not the equivalents of the lutanists of England, Italy, Germany and France. They were a separate species, and in the latter league were a number of Spanish lutanists, though these tended to be overshadowed by the men with the *vihuela.*

Milán, as the leading figure in the world of the *vihuela,* was in some respects the Spanish counterpart of the Englishman John Dowland. Although Dowland was the more profound composer, and, contrary to the popular idea of reticent Englishmen and demonstrative Latins, the more melancholy and emotional artist, Milán was not inferior in invention and originality in his own domain. Again, the analogy should not be pushed too far; but the correspondence between the Spanish and English musical worlds of the period has to be remarked— two powerful nations at loggerheads overlapping and complementing each other in music and the arts. It remains an interesting and perhaps significant touch of historic irony.

The most important figure of the period in concerted instrumental music was Diego Ortiz whose important early work on thorough bass, *A Tratado de Glosas,* was published in Rome in 1553. Ortiz was a highly talented and inventive composer of Recercadas or 'divisions' (Italian, Ricercare, though there are aesthetic and linguistic variants; in this sense variations on a ground, but in others 'fugue with art'). These works are of considerable beauty and expressiveness as well as being pioneer examples of their genre, technically resourceful.

So far Spanish music, sacred and secular, vocal and instrumental, has developed and retained an innate character of its own, a recognizably Spanish quality. There are 'foreign' influences, naturally; no civilized country or society exists in either a material or a spiritual vacuum, and although the Spanish sense of pride of race and its destiny remained strong, the isolation at the hands of history and geography which characterized the national outlook was never complete or intended so to be; and in the arts it was in a paradoxical way including rather than excluding in its effects.

Spain was one of the leaders in revitalization of the arts of the fifteenth and sixteenth centuries: it was one of Spain's great periods, with literature, drama and painting as well as music flourishing with the overall national sense of power and destined greatness. The Renaissance has long been recognized as the great evolutionary thrust forward of Western civilization, the age in which the Christian soul became acutely aware of the will to create, even though many of its leading figures were either declared agnostics or outright atheists. Indeed, a kind of obstinate agnosticism was inherent in the Renaissance man's struggle for liberation from the old monastic life—and its values. But it was in another sense a great movement of the Christian world, and, in the Counter-Reformation in particular, Spain took the leading role, and in many ways the consciously upholding role. In the sense that it was truly a time when the Christian soul awoke to awareness of its full creative potential, the sixteenth century was Spain's peak and glory.

But the Renaissance was ultimately, in the words of the Russian philosopher Nicholas Berdyaev, 'the most sublime, significant and tragic failure ever experienced by European man'. This failure and its consequences struck particularly hard in Spain; but it is still not clear why those consequences should have been so far-ranging and damaging, on the surface more than anywhere else in Europe. So the question has to be asked: Was Spain's national 'decline' during the subsequent centuries a direct consequence of the failure of the Renaissance or was it due to some other, inherent, and specifically Spanish cause? Put like that it is probably too simplistic and too disingenuous; yet the essence of the matter may still lie in such a question or one similar to it.

The reasons for the Spanish decline, which took the national but not the popular music with it, are difficult to define and analyse, as we have seen. The commonplace idea is that it was a direct consequence of the activities of the Inquisition. But that really does not hold water: the Inquisition was neither uniquely Spanish nor particularly severe in Spain. It was a Roman institution formally established by Pope Gregory IX in 1235, and was more strictly and rigorously applied in Italy and sometimes in France. True, there was a Spanish form of it established in 1478 by Pope Sixtus IV which, though nominally under papal control, was in reality at the service of the Spanish State. But its interference in Spanish affairs generally did not have a more inhibiting effect than elsewhere. It had its specifically Spanish characteristics and was determined in detail by the nature of Spanish society, the cast of the Spanish mind and the particular structure of Spain as a socio-political unity. And indeed, that was part of the difficulty: Spanish national unity was comparatively new and in many ways still precarious. Thus the use of the Inquisition for political as well as religious ends tended to extend through the entire social structure, bearing particularly heavily on dissenting elements.

Yet even here the case is not as straightforward as it is usually presented: for example, Jews and Moors were not molested by the Inquisition as Jews or Moors but because they were lapsed Catholics. And if it appeared to bear particularly on the English and on English sailors captured in the long running wars between Spain and England, that was almost entirely because of Catholic Spain's determination, also seen as a command of destiny, to bring the heretical nation of Henry VIII and Elizabeth I back into the fold. The English Protestants were to contemporary Spaniards the worst of heretics, and this tended to bear more heavily than the political fact that they were Spain's enemies. Indeed, the way in which to Anglo-Saxon ears the term 'Spanish Inquisition' evokes images of exceptional cruelty and repression, an idea of tyranny and persecution hardly equalled by the worst excesses of the French Revolution and only exceeded by the outrages of Nazi Germany, is almost entirely due to the intensity of the feud between Spain and England in the sixteenth century, a feud all the more bitter and intense because of its religious bias.

Yet this same period saw the peak of Spanish arts and world-wide achievements: for a nation toiling under a repressive tyranny the production in all fields was remarkable. The 'Black Legend' of the Spanish Inquisition, understandable where historical memory is long and prejudice deep ingrained, will not bear objective scrutiny.

The Inquisition, in Spain and elsewhere, was in many ways iniquitous, though it was probably no more so than all established authorities of the time. But in Spain it did have one added disadvantage: it dragged on long after it was suppressed elsewhere and after its usefulness was spent, its purpose outrun. In France the Inquisition was suppressed in 1772; in Spain it lingered on until 1808, and its successor, the Tribunal of Faith, until 1834. And, as is the invariable rule, the latter stages of any once viable institution are the worst, the most rigid, the most stultifying. It was so with the Spanish Inquisition: during its final years it had a more inhibiting effect than it ever had when it was at its height and the true expression of the national consciousness, and enjoyed massive popular support.

How much this hanging on to an outworn institution was the result of tenacity on the part of the Inquisition itself and how much to a kind of national ossification which culminated in a resistance to all new ideas, whether in the area of religion or not, is a pretty question. Almost certainly it was a combination of both. But what is clear is that during the later years of the Inquisition and all the years of the Tribunal of Faith, Spain retreated into a kind of obstructionist backwater; and whether it was a result of the Inquisition's longevity or the cause of it is another of those questions which are so interrelated that no decisive answer is possible.

But whatever effects the Inquisition may have had on the national life as a whole, it had little to do with the musical decline—except in so far as any nation's artistic productions are the expressions of its deepest and most autonomous national consciousness. In any case, it is necessary to speak of the Spanish 'decline' after the Golden Century with caution. The Spaniards themselves, while acknowledging it as historical fact in a general sense, tend to put a somewhat different interpretation on it from that of outsiders.

Today the Spaniards still retain that old view of themselves as apart from the rest of Europe, not in the sense that the English despite EEC membership, are still basically insular and parochial, but as the historic preservers of Catholic Latin civilization. In the true Spanish world- and life-view, both changing and unchanging through the centuries, is to be found the key to the historical evolution and to the innermost nature of Spanish art forms.

Thus the so-called Spanish 'decline' is ethnologically relative and ontologically suspect. And certainly Spanish popular life, and with it popular music, retained an innate vigour and distinction even through the politically and internationally barren years. Neither political fallibility nor economic weakness could destroy the natural vitality and ingrained pride and passion of the Spanish people. Nor did foreign rule and a far from indigenous court do more than gild the surface. Underneath Spain remained totally and inescapably Spain, a strong current of natural life and vitality maintained. And it was from this sturdy natural current that the musical revival sprang in the first place, where the 'renaissance' was born.

But there was a long interregnum between the glory of the Golden Age and the consolidation of the 'renaissance'; the period of foreign domination when the native voice was largely but not entirely subdued to alien influences, mostly Italian, outside the popular idioms.

It would be an exaggeration to say that the Italianization of Spanish music was caused by Domenico Scarlatti. Yet Scarlatti's influence was far reaching and in many respects beyond definition. Born in Naples in 1685 (a ripe year for musical births since it included also Bach and Handel), he was the son of Alessandro Scarlatti, the influential pioneer of Italian opera. In his youth Domenico followed broadly his father's style and production; but in 1721 he went to Lisbon as music master teacher to the Infanta María Magdalena Barbara de Braganza, and when María Barbara married the second son of Philip V of Spain who succeeded him as Ferdinand VI, Scarlatti accompanied her to Madrid. At that time there were many Neapolitans in Madrid, on account of Spanish rule in Naples, and Scarlatti found himself in a thoroughly congenial atmosphere. Also, Spain under Ferdinand VI began to regain some of the prosperity she had lost when Philip II died leaving her bankrupt and exhausted. Intellectually and artistically too Spain recovered much under Ferdinand. Never again was she to reach the heights of the Golden Century; but a certain stability and confidence returned so that all who worked in the capital during those early years of the eighteenth century had some solid foundations to build on.

Scarlatti lived in Madrid in the royal service for the rest of his life, until he died in 1757; and it was during those years that he composed most of his famous series of more than 500 *Eserczi*, or sonatas, those immensely alive and inventive works for harpsichord which not only paved the way for the evolution of classical sonata form, but exercised a huge influence both on the art music of Spain and on keyboard playing and composition everywhere. Ironic at first sight is the way in which the leading composers of the renaissance over a century later, notably Falla himself, who were in the habit of denouncing the Italian influence on Spanish music and its debilitating effects on the native product, themselves looked to Scarlatti as mentor and exemplar.

The Spanish influence on Scarlatti's music has always been recognized: the sonatas are full of the sound of guitars, the clack of castanets, of the echo of stamping feet, of melodic turns specifically Spanish, of indigenous rhythms and dance measures. But modern scholarship has demonstrated conclusively and in detail that the great majority of the sonatas are based upon authentic Spanish tunes which can be and have been identified. The leading authority in this field is the English harpsichordist Jane Clarke, wife of the composer Stephen Dodgson, whose work has opened up entirely new perspectives and thrown fresh light on Scarlatti's relationship to Spanish music. Maybe Falla and the other composers of his time knew what has only become clear to us in recent years.

35

Scarlatti's contribution to the evolution of sonata form, strengthened by Gerstenberg's recognition of the 'pairings', is relevant to a general rather than a specific musical study; but his influence on the specific (Spanish) field is in itself both remarkable and illuminating.

One of the most gifted and certainly the most famous of Scarlatti's Spanish disciples was Padre Antonio Soler who was born in 1729 and died at Escorial in 1783. Soler, a noted theorist and musical historian as well as composer, enjoyed the patronage of the Infante Don Gabriel, younger brother of Charles IV. His theoretical treatise *Llave de la modulación y antiguedades*, published in Madrid in 1762, was important and influential and sets forth his own rules of composition. As a composer Soler was prolific in vocal and chamber music as well as the keyboard concertos and sonatas for which he is best remembered today and which show the influence of Scarlatti at its best and most creative. There is no doubt that had his music, especially his keyboard music, been as well known during the nineteenth century as it has become in the twentieth, his influence on the renaissance of Spanish music would have been far greater, probably as great as that of Scarlatti himself.

The Scarlatti tradition of keyboard music survived into the nineteenth century and through to the beginning of the twentieth, though in a modified and often weakened form, in the hands of composers such as Mateo Albéniz.

The real evidence of musical decline which cannot be evaded or avoided lies in the music of the theatre where the debilitated Italian influence pervaded even the native form of the *zarzuela*. At its strongest in the mid-eighteenth century Italian opera took over Madrid entirely and a number of Italian musicians settled there and produced works of varying quality and accomplishment. However, as the century wore on political and social changes made the Spanish capital less inviting, and many of the Italians left. But the legacy was damaging: the ubiquity of Italian opera in Spain effectively prevented the growth of any true national opera outside the *zarzuela* theatre. In one sense the Italian dominance encouraged the growth of the *zarzuela* as the only indigenous form in the lyric theatre, even though at one time the Italian domination was so complete that even the *zarzuela* writers gave up trying. Indeed, at one time during this period, the *zarzuela* yielded in popular favour to the developing *tonadilla escénicas*, a kind of miniature theatrical entertainment lasting from about ten to twenty minutes depending on the number of performers. There was also the *tonadilla* as solo song, or *tonada*, originating in Castile and often satirical in tone. Granados's well-known set represents a modern extension of an old form. The insidious Italian influence on the *zarzuela* did not come until later; but its debilitating effects on the Spanish musical theatre in general dates from the time when the Italians first ruled Madrid and then went home leaving a kind of vacuum.

Another Italian, Luigi Boccherini, also settled in Madrid, originally under the patronage of Prince Louis, Charles IV's uncle; but although he too absorbed much of the Spanish flavour and temper into his music, his influence was not great. Boccherini's part in the story is confined to instrumental compositions, for chamber music and guitar principally, and does not range farther, certainly not into the field of opera.

Either end of the nineteenth century Spanish music suffered severe loss through the early deaths of two composers of real talent running to potential genius. Both were Basques and both might have altered the longer perspectives of Spanish music, especially Spanish opera. As it was, fate decided otherwise so the story of Spanish music is left with a pair of might-have-beens in some ways analogous to that facing the student of English music with the early death of Purcell. Neither Spaniard had time to reveal a quality of genius equal to Purcell's; but Purcell lived a few years longer than either and, in one of the Spanish cases at least, the evidence points to virtually unlimited possibilities.

Juan Crisóstimos Arriaga died in Paris in January 1806, barely twenty years old. He already had several notable compositions to his name, including three string quartets and a symphony. There are obvious 'influences' at work in Arriaga's music, Beethoven and Haydn principally but Weber and Schubert also, as one would expect in a boy striking out to find his own voice; and that voice is readily discerned behind the influences and echoes, even in the opera *Los esclavos felices* written when he was only fourteen (the overture at least remains current). He was born to the day 50 years after Mozart, and such was his quick promise and embryonic achievement that well before his death he was being likened to that incomparable master.

But if Arriaga was strong in talent, he was congenitally weak in health: the cause of his death, sometimes euphemistically put down to 'decline', was almost certainly consumption, probably ingenerate. Since he came when Spanish music badly needed a native genius to set it on its new path into a new century, Arriaga's early death was a tragedy that had far-ranging if indefinable effects.

José María Usandizaga managed to live seven years longer than Arriaga and didn't die until 90 years after that ill-fated young man. He was thus born into the 'renaissance' and died in the middle of it. He composed several operas of which *Las Golondrinas* (The Swallows) is probably the best known and shows a talent clearly capable of development and extension. Its subject of love and jealousy among a group of travelling players is similar to that of *I Pagliacci*: it is less robust than that noisy piece of business but touches a more sensitive and deeper vein of lyricism. If Usandizaga had lived he might well have not only exercised a major influence on the Spanish musical theatre, bridging the gap between operetta (or *zarzuela*) and opera proper, but have founded a school of Spanish opera which has never materialized despite the occasional enduring example such as *La vida breve* and *Goyescas*. As it is, Usandizaga's theatre works hover somewhere between opera and operetta. These include *Mendi-Mendiyan* and *La Llama* as well as *Las Golondrinas*. There is no doubt that a longer life would have drawn from him an extended and strengthened list of theatrical compositions. What he did compose achieves much and promises more. It is not wanting in artistic direction; but the impression remains that his talent was still only in its formative stages at the time of his death.

Between the shooting and falling stars of Arriaga and Usandizaga, through the body of the nineteenth century, came the consolidation of the *zarzuela* as the foremost genre of the musical theatre in Spain and the conception and birth of the

Spanish musical renaissance led by Felipe Pedrell and consolidated by Manuel de Falla and others. In the compositions
of Falla above all the true voice and spirit of the Spanish
nation was recovered and projected out into the mainstream
of European music. It is not quite a matter of full circle,
Victoria to Falla; but nothing in Spanish music after Victoria
spoke for eternal Spain in real depth and power until the
mature works of Falla. If the outer voice is different, the
inner spirit is in true conjunction. And the coincidence with
English music and its own renaissance remains: Morales and
Victoria to Falla and Granados; Tallis and Byrd to Elgar and
Vaughan Williams: the pattern persists and does not rest there.
The points of divergence are no less illuminating; the soil
and the seed produced a contemporaneous crop in and under
differing social and ethnic conditions. If history does not
repeat itself in detail, it usually pays attention to essentials
and does not neglect necessary lines of individual and multiple
evolution.

II

THE ZARZUELA SYNDROME

THE THREE MOST characteristic sounds of Spanish music are: the organs of the great Spanish cathedrals with their banks of *trompetas reales*; the composite sounds of flamenco, specifically *cante jondo*; and the orchestra, chorus and aria of the *zarzuela*. Serious Spanish musicians will no doubt still object to such a contention, at least in the second and third categories—the marvellous Spanish organs do not seem to have come into the argument either way: many have fallen into neglect, though work of restoration has been undertaken in a number of cases. But flamenco and *zarzuela* were looked down upon by the musical idealists and propagandists who instigated the renaissance around the turn of the century. This is to some extent understandable, certainly in the case of *zarzuela*, which has always been a local, domestic, inward-looking form. But the progenitors of the renaissance were looking outward towards the larger world, striving to break out of the parochialism and localism of too much Spanish popular music and so to project a national art form into the mainstream of European music. And this in fact is the crux of the problem, not only for the Spanish nationalist, but for all proponents of a national art that seeks broader vistas.

The distinction between a folk art and a national art is crucial: a folk art has a domestic, localized aim and appeal; a national art a universal, objective one. It is a difference that is by no means always sufficiently marked: a great deal of confusion exists because folk art is not distinguished from true national art and *vice versa*, so that the proper standards of judgement and reference are not applied and both aims and achievements in consequence become distorted. The truly national artist is always more completely attuned to the national spirit in all its facets and varieties than the mere folk or domestic artist, though that tuning and the emotional and intellectual penetration it postulates are less obvious and usually less widely appreciated. For the Spanish national composer the danger of confusion of aim and application has always been greater and more tempting: the particular stamp and character of Spanish popular music is superficially more obvious than almost any other and therefore more easily purloined for musical counterfeiting or merely picturesque evocations of no lasting worth or importance.

Yet by no means all folk art is irrelevant or to be seen as counterfeit when used in an artistic setting with genuinely national intentions. The dividing line is not clear and precise, and in addition the folk art often has a valuable rôle in germinating the national production from within. On the other hand, that rôle must remain one of germination only: no major national composer uses, or has used, folk material itself in any quantity; it is the informing spirit that matters. Nor is it only those countries with a strong and continuous musical tradition that can draw fruitfully on a folk heritage. The relationship of Haydn's thematic material to Austrian and Croatian folk tunes is a fascinating and inexhaustible subject, while Brahms's claim that whenever he was stuck for a melody he would think of some German folk song tells us more about him and his creative faculty than any number of theoretical analyses. The manner in which Brahms's music is constantly fertilized from German folk music while Wagner's hardly ever reveals more about both and the 'clash' of artistic aims and temperaments than all the querulous sniping around the 'New Music' and 'tradition' that made the mid-nineteenth century in Germany musically ridiculous.

Flamenco and *zarzuela*, each in its own fashion, sometimes in complementary and sometimes in separate operation, helped fertilize the creative processes that informed and consolidated the Spanish musical renaissance, alongside the old liturgical music and the courtly and Romanesque art of the Middle Ages, rediscovered during the latter part of the last century. But, as we have seen, the 'serious' composers and scholars had little time for the *zarzuela* in particular, which they regarded as frivolous and shallow as they regarded flamenco as coarse and vulgar. There was truth in both assumptions, given the standpoint of those who held to them: much of the music from the *zarzuela* theatre was trivial and derivative, and a good deal of flamenco was both coarse-grained and spurious. But at the heart of each was a hard core of genuine Spanish feeling and character which, when creatively transformed, if not inevitably sublimated, went and had to go into the making of the new Spanish music.

The position of the great Spanish organs was different. They appeared to interest few if any of the younger musicians. Yet their special character, in particular their *trompetas reales*, produce a sound that is spectacularly strident and totally Spanish, in many respects a kind of parallel with the flamenco singer's nasal melismas on the one hand and with the 'tough' scoring for wind and brass in the *zarzuela* orchestra on the other. The magnificent instrument in Toledo Cathedral known as 'The Emperor's Organ', with its curved banks of *trompetas* fanning outwards across the width of the building, is one of the supreme examples of the typical Spanish organ. (There are in fact two other fine organs in Toledo Cathedral, as well as superb ones in other cathedral towns, notably Segovia.) The Toledo organ has been restored and sounds magnificent, producing as it does a blend and power of tones to lift and ring in proud and imperious praise of God and State. The *trompetas reales* are not the only distinguishing tonal quality of Spanish organs: their special blend of reeds and mixtures and mutations is remarkable; and it should not be forgotten that it was in Spain that the first advocacy of equal tempera-ment for the organ originated when Don Ramis de Pareja, a learned musician who was born in Baeza, Andalucía, *c.* 1440, argued in favour of equal temperament and so began a con-troversy that lasted for several centuries as the diehards struggled to maintain the old system, regarded as sacrosanct in its day, against the new-fangled idea. Equal temperament of course won out in the end, as it had to; but the battle was long and bitter: there is nothing more formidable than a Spanish diehard.

All the same, it is those superb reed stops, the *trompetas reales* (which can mean both 'real' and 'royal' trumpets) which distinguish Spanish organs from all others and in particular set them apart from Schnitgers and Silbermanns of Central Europe. But if these characteristic stops set the Spanish organs apart, they no less confirm their typification of the overall Spanish musical soundpicture, linked to aspects of that picture as diverse as flamenco, *zarzuela* and the great tradition of Spanish liturgical music. If the *clarines* seem to have something of the nasal quality of the flamenco singer, the *magnas* reflect the strong chest tones of the characteristic Spanish vocal production in opera and *zarzuela—trompetas reales* situated somewhere around the breastbone.

Although the *zarzuela* is generally thought of as an essentially nineteenth-century manifestation, in fact its origins go much farther back, to the seventeenth century and the period of classic drama in the time of Calderón. The first work to be definitely called *zarzuela* was a mythological concoction entitled *El golfo de Apolo de las Sirenas*, staged in 1657. In its early form the *zarzuela* was a basically serious entertainment resembling the court masque, with frequent mythological trappings and few of the deliberate comicalities or satirical asides that were to become its major features later on. Most of the music of the early *zarzuelas* is lost or unknown, and with the domination of the Italian opera style in the eighteenth century, it soon lost its inherent character and clear direction. The name *zarzuela*, incidentally, derives from the royal palace or hunting lodge outside Madrid, recently restored and used by the present Spanish royal family, where these entertainments originally took place. The word itself stems from a particular type of bramble which grew and proliferated outside Madrid and was named *zarza*.

The regeneration of the *zarzuela* which took place in the mid-nineteenth century was in part at least a conscious reaction against the Italian domination in opera. It thus began by going back to the earlier roots in the Calderón period. In a sense, here was a beginning of a renaissance in advance of the actual one instigated by Pedrell and consolidated by his disciples, even though it took initial impetus from the very source that later came to be despised.

One of the principal aims of the composers of the rejuvenated

43

zarzuela was to 'de-Italianize' Spanish opera, and in this its leading composer, though by no means the only one, was Francisco Barbieri who found his native voice with *Jugar con fuego* (1851) and finally consolidated it with *El barberillo de Lavapies* (1874). This was the real beginning of the *zarzuela* as it evolved through the nineteenth century and into the twentieth as the completely *echt*-Spanish genre in the musical theatre. In between writing *zarzuelas* Barbieri was active as a composer of other forms and as a musical administrator. In the latter capacity he was responsible for bringing much unfamiliar music to the Spanish public through the Sociedad de Conciertos de Madrid, which he had founded in 1866. That these 'unfamiliar' works included the major symphonies of Beethoven indicates how backward and out of touch musical appreciation in Spain had become. Regrettably, the same tends to be so today, with the average musical audience reactionary and frequently obstructionist, at best unadventurous in Madrid, though the situation in Barcelona appears to be somewhat better.

The first phase of the *zarzuela* revival was marked by a strong *castizo* feeling, that is by a return to the roots and a precision of style, linked both by nature and deliberate association to the eighteenth-century evocations of popular Madrileño life as depicted by Goya and the musical 'purity' of Scarlatti. Certainly the *zarzuelas* of Barbieri and his colleagues were essentially local and domestic Spanish productions, emphasized by the rejection of the Italian cosmopolitan style. But they still played their part in re-establishing the authentic Spanish voice in music and in their way led on to the renaissance itself. However they and their successors may have seemed trivial and frivolous to the propagandists and idealists of the renaissance, and justly so in many of the later cases, it remains true that a genuinely national art has to begin from a local and domestic one, and these *zarzuelas* gave, in one aspect, the impetus towards the creation of a new Spanish national music. Pedrell himself sought primary inspiration for the revival in popular and folk music, as well as in the old court and liturgical works; Barbieri and his companions and successors sought it no less in the popular life of the capital, cosmopolitan as well as national, varied, vivid, no less indigenous and no less essential.

But despite the efforts of Barbieri and those who believed in and worked with him—notably Gaztambide, who was one of several musicians to co-operate with Barbieri in founding the Teatro de la Zarzuela in Madrid in 1856, as well as Outrid and Torregosa—the Italian influence continued to dominate the musical theatre in Spain. It was a younger man, Tomás Bretón, who produced the major classic of the later *zarzuela* style. *La Verbena de la Paloma* (The Festival of the Dove) not only achieved spectacular success in Spain and South America but, more important, established a new genre for the lyric theatre. *La Verbena* is an undoubted masterpiece, full of authentic Spanish life and vitality in its depiction of the Madrileño customs and activities, and full too of rich comedy and a quick-running satire. Bretón was in several respects the Spanish equivalent of Arthur Sullivan, a man and musician of serious mind and intention who aspired to make his primary mark in grand opera (in Sullivan's case in oratorio as well) and the other forms of 'serious' composition, but who ultimately found his fame and fortune in the comic lyric theatre. Bretón wrote many other theatrical works, probably the best known being *La Dolores*, as well as the full opera *Guzman el bueno*, infrequently heard now but important in the evolution of Bretón's genius. But *La Verbena* is his classic masterpiece of *zarzuela* and remains to justify the entire genre in the face of all slighting criticism.

La Verbena de la Paloma, which has at least two additional titles or names deriving from various aspects of its subject and its treatment, devolves round the La Latina quarter of Madrid with its fiesta of the Virgin of the Dove, the patron saint of the capital. It is, as its titles intimate, a many-sided work; but the heart remains the true evocation of Madrid life and customs.

The three classics of the modern-style *zarzuela* which came to fruition in the 1890s, are *La Verbena de la Paloma*, Chapí's *La Revoltosa* (The Lady Rebel) and Chueca's *Agua, azucarillos y aguardiente* (virtually untranslatable, certainly with its apt alliterations, but perhaps best rendered by the American

45

Water, candy and brandy). Federico Chueca was in some respects the most gifted of all the classic *zarzuela* composers. He was the only one admired by Falla, and it is not difficult to see why. Although on the surface Chueca's *zarzuela* music—other examples are *La Gran Via*, a semi-revue-style piece revolving round the opening of Madrid's main thoroughfare in 1886, and *La alegría de la huerte* (Fun and games in the orchard)—appears somewhat coarse and rowdy, if full of character, on another level it is probably the most authentically Spanish of all, and touches the exposed Spanish nerve in a way many of the more apparently polished and sophisticated scores do not. It is essentially archetypal.

If Bretón was a serious musician of great integrity who took immense pains over everything he did, and Chueca was also a highly imaginative craftsman who knew exactly what he wanted to do and did it without compromise or inhibition, Ruperto Chapí was more easy going, inclined to put top-class work alongside more slapdash production. Chapí, to be sure, was always a sincere artist, and perhaps 'slapdash' is too strong a word; yet several of Chapí's scores seem not to have come from any imperative conviction so much as from a good habit of work and an easy acceptance of the conventions. His three-Act *La Tempestad* (The Storm) is carefully made but somewhat nebulous: as with most *zarzuela*-type works set outside Spain, the essential character seems to suffer, no doubt inevitably for the aim can no longer be precise and specific. If the central idea is the Spanish temperament and character in action, as in the true *zarzuela*, then everything that lies outside Spain is not true grist to the mill; but if a larger, international conception is intended, than a broader, more universal, less localized style is required. There is no doubt a certain paradox here; but if the pursuit of a rejuvenated national or continental art form is sought, then the inevitable paradoxes have to be faced and accepted.

La Tempestad is set in a Breton fishing village: it contains pleasant music, well-enough written, but not more so than any number of agreeably inoffensive operettas with no particular ring of time or place: like Pablo Luna's *Molinos de Viento* (Windmills) set in Holland, *La Tempestad* lacks the stamp and hall-mark of the true *zarzuela*. That Chapí was capable of writing the true type and style is proved not only by *La Revoltosa*, but by such an irresistible piece as *El Barquillero* (The Wafer Seller) with its entrancing chorus of wafer sellers at the end, pure *zarzuela* and pure Madrileño.

The big three classic *zarzuelas*, *La Verbena de la Paloma*, *La Revoltosa* and *Agua, azucarillos y aguardiente* all centre on Madrid life and customs. And indeed, it could be argued that the true *zarzuela* is essentially a Madrileño affair. Yet one of the best and most popular of all, Caballero's *Gigantes y Cabezudos* (Giants and Bigheads), is set in Aragón and is devoted to Aragonese life, the jota prominent. It is no wonder that this has been claimed as the most popular of all *zarzuelas*. In its general guying of bureaucratic bigheadedness at a time when the Spanish defeats in Cuba were smarting and could be seen as a puncturing of the bubble of presumptuous authority and its legendary incompetence, it represents a permanent Spanish theme. Caballero wrote several first-class *zarzuelas* besides *Gigantes y Cabezudos*, among the most celebrated being *El Duo de La Africana* (a tale of rivalries and jealousies backstage during a performance of Meyerbeer's *L'Africaine*) and *La Viejecita* (The Little Old Lady), and so must be regarded as one of the leaders of the genre. Aragón has inspired a number of other *zarzuelas*, such as José Serrano's *Los de Aragón* (The Aragonese), a pleasant piece if without the character of *Gigantes y Cabezudos*; but it does further indicate how the *zarzuela* travels happily outside Madrid and into the Spanish provinces, though not outside the borders of Spain itself.

The authentic *zarzuela* of customs and character, the *zarzuela chico*, is a corporate affair, in which the speaking characters (who may not sing at all) gag with the audience as well as with each other, and the whole thing tends to be topical and irreverent (though attempts to 'up date' the jokes usually do little more than undermine the atmosphere). The lines between and dividing revue, comic opera and operetta in *zarzuela* are frequently blurred; but the heart of the matter lies in the essential Spanishness, whatever the nomenclature. The trouble often arises when that essential Spanishness is subdued to a more refined or 'respectable' musical style, again Italian

47

orientated, in an effort to attract the foreign ear (or maybe simply from lack of any distinctive native talent), or when ambition outreaches ability and so results in a confusion of aims and means. One of the most gifted of the later composers for the Spanish theatre, Amadeo Vives (1871–1932), produced in *Doña Francisquita* a lyric comedy of immense charm and attractiveness, the equal at least of all but the outright masterpieces of the Viennese or Parisian operetta schools, and the superior of most. But many of his other works for the stage, *Maruxa* and *Bohemios* for example, reveal little more than pallid competence, lacking all the qualities that make the Spanish musical theatre and give it distinction. Federico Moreno Torroba (born 1891), a still later musician carried competence a lot farther and produced a number of works of first-rate light quality, of which *Luisa Fernanda* is probably the the best—and excellent it is. But compositions of this kind, which really belong not to the *chico* genre but to that known as the *zarzuela grande*, have moved a fair way from the classic form of the 1890s and only at their very best maintain the incisive national character. Much else showed evidence of triviality and a lack of true seriousness, which must never be confused with solemnity for there are half a dozen and more solemn works to every truly serious one, and not only in this context: in every context.

There is no call here to catalogue all the quality *zarzuelas* and their composers: the main lines are all that signify and these have been indicated, though it should not be forgotten that in performance *zarzuela* has always been a vehicle for the best singers and orchestral musicians, by no means a refuge for the musically mediocre in any sense. So the question arises again: Why did Falla and the idealists of the renaissance affect to despise the *zarzuela* and all it stood for, especially since at its best it was both the forerunner of the renaissance and the repository of all that was left in the theatre of any form of Spanish musical tradition and authentic national tone during the barren years?

Part of the answer, as we have seen, lies in the way the *zarzuela* was seen, correctly, as purely local and domestic; another part in the triviality of many of the second-line scores.

Yet at the deeper level there was an inevitable feeling that a vigorous national music had to be based upon stronger foundations; that the *zarzuela*, however spicy, attractive and at its best worthwhile it might be, was a barrier to such a revival rather than a spur to it. Again, that feeling is understandable in the context: it may have been shortsighted, but idealists and enthusiasts intent upon a particular goal and set on a particular course are often wanting in breadth of vision and, of a certain inner necessity, are propelled from within a long narrow and, in the general sense, inflexible path. If there had been even a subdued current of serious Spanish national composition at the time of the first stirrings of the revival, the *zarzuela* might have been seen in a different light and a broader perspective. As it was, it could be regarded not only as a limiting factor in the nationalist context, but still worse as a trap, a snare and a temptation wherein composers who might have contributed to the real renaissance were sidetracked into dalliance with the *zarzuela* as the quick road to fame and fortune. Such a one was Amadeo Vives who, whatever his real achievements, was seen as a loss to the serious cause; and such another was even Tomás Bretón himself whose dreams of founding a flourishing Spanish grand opera were undermined by the enormous success of his *zarzuelas*.

Inevitably, the attractions of *zarzuela* proved and continued insidious. The composer's lot is seldom a prosperous one even in the best of times, and the chance of fame in the theatre is hard to resist by all but the sternest minds.

Yet even these, under pressure as they frequently are by the force of circumstances, are not always sufficient. Falla himself, in want of money and encouragement as a young man and not yet in possession of a sophisticated and personalized technique, turned his hand to the *zarzuela*. It was a decision taken without enthusiasm and solely for material ends. And it was not attended by success. Yet the very fact of it shows how deep was the influence of *zarzuela* and how a kind of love-hate relationship could develop between it and the most serious-minded composer. Of the five* *zarzuelas* Falla did compose, only one, *Los Amores de la Iñes*, was ever performed

* See Appendix I

49

in public. Falla, in his own judgement, regarded another, *La Casa de Tócame Roque*, as the only one in any sense worthy of bearing his name, and it is the one which is linked by a curious coincidence with Federico Chueca. It seems that Chueca wanted to help his young friend and so let it be rumoured that he had co-operated in *La Casa*, in the hope that the supposed association would commend the piece to theatrical managers. It did not work out as hoped; on the other hand, it did lead to other rumours that Falla had taken a hand in the orchestration of some of Chueca's own *zarzuelas*. It was all fantasy and speculation; but it does throw a minor sidelight onto the musical world and the artistic circumstances in which Falla struggled to find his own creative voice and grow to artistic maturity.

I have said that one of the three classic *zarzuelas* of the 1890s' highpoint is Chapí's *La Revoltosa*. The librettist of that piece was Carlos Fernández Shaw, a prolific writer for the *zarzuela* theatre, a good poet and an influential editor. He was librettist for some of the best works of the Spanish lyric and comic theatre, not only in the *chico* but also in the *grande* style. Among the outstanding works on which he co-operated were Vives's *Doña Francisquita*, Torroba's *Luisa Fernanda*, Jesús Guridi's excellent three-acter on Basque themes *El Caserío* (in Basque *Caserui*) and Serrano's *La Canción del Olvido* (The Song of Forgetfulness), a work of considerable accomplishment but no great character. Thus Shaw was an experienced librettist (the above is only a short list of his contributions) in a variety of contexts, by no means confined to the comic and 'revue' type of theatre productions.

It is therefore difficult to accept the view that away from the *chico* style of *zarzuela* with its bias towards comedy and fairly obvious intrigue, Shaw was out of his depth. And this assumes particular significance because he was the librettist for Falla's opera *La vida breve* and the dramatic weakness of that work has frequently been laid to his charge. This is no doubt true up to a point; but it was almost certainly from choice, a deliberate concept, rather than from a lack of the ability to write otherwise. This collaboration between the most gifted and experienced *zarzuela* librettist and the rising young composer who had yet to establish his reputation and mature his technique, has a specific importance in the evolution of Spanish national music as it aspired to spread outwards in its basic appeal but draw also upon the international mainstream for its nurturing.

La vida breve, the earliest of his compositions Falla wished to acknowledge, has for all its surface charm and local atmosphere a hard core of musical method, a latent intellectual severity which sets it apart from all other Spanish works for the musical theatre of the period. And it has nothing whatever to do with the *zarzuela* tradition to which it has, by some commentators, been carelessly linked. That tradition depends almost exclusively upon domestic colour and picturesque popular elements of a kind Falla was from now on determined to avoid. He had already absorbed as much of those as he would ever need; and in any case, the racy humour, the juicy gusto and frequent eruptions of raffish satire of the best of the *zarzuelas* never found an echo in Falla's austere, frequently ascetic world- and life-view, here or elsewhere. His aims and objectives were different, and never again would he deviate from his self-set course.

La vida breve is by no means fully characteristic of Falla's genius; but it does indicate at several points the ultimate direction his maturing artistry was to take. True, it is dramatically ineffectual: the story is too static and contains too little inner tension and confrontation of developed character. Thus in one sense Falla began with what looked like a major handicap. From the point of view of the theatre, *La vida breve* gets nowhere. Nothing in particular 'happens' (but then nothing much 'happens' in *Tristan und Isolde* either). Yet the inconclusive dramatic structure did offer Falla opportunities to work out a musical setting in which the evocation of atmosphere and the exploitation of sub-principal elements could be given particular importance. And this, at the time of *La vida breve*'s composition was precisely what he needed. He may have hinted as much to Shaw, whom he deliberately sought out as his librettist, when the subject was first mooted and discussed between them. The swift transitions, the necessity for sharp characterizations, the constant shift of timing and emphasis

51

necessary to truly effective drama or the comedy or divertise-
ment of manners—these might well have demanded of Falla a
particular skill he did not at the time possess or had not yet
mastered. The very 'limitations' of the libretto, such as they
were, probably helped rather than hindered him. Experience
and evidence show that Shaw was perfectly capable of producing another kind of libretto had it been required of him,
and that his understanding of human beings in contexts other
than that of *zarzuela chico* was by no means as shallow as it is
often suggested.

Musically, too, *La vida breve* is frequently derivative. This
is especially true of the formal operatic numbers, the set
pieces such as the Love Duet and the Trio in Act II; even to
a certain extent of the two celebrated arias for soprano.
Behind and beneath the obviously Spanish turns of phrase
and placing of accent, the influence of Massenet and Puccini,
even of the Wagner of *Tristan*, shows through. All the same,
these alien influences and echoes were no more than incidental:
in the recitatives and the orchestral interludes and the two
'Dances', *La vida breve* struck a new note in opera, and it was
an indigenously Spanish note with a direct response to the
inflexions of the Spanish language. And already, those 'cadence
harmonies' which were to play a major part in defining
Falla's later style are in evidence.

The originality of *La vida breve* does not, as I say, lie in its
set pieces and formal operatic assumptions. It comes in the
profound evocations of poetic atmosphere and in the authenticity of the Andalucían setting—in the musical backcloth, so
to speak. This setting, or backcloth, is wholly original in
execution as well as in conception; and by another aspect of
the paradox the very authenticity of the Andalucían setting
passes beyond the merely folk and local and projects the art
into the realm of the truly national and from there to the
universal. The first bars of all are at once individual and
authoritative; and the succeeding chorus depicting the black-
smiths at work in Granada and cursing the harshness of their
lot (also a flamenco motif) is both dramatically effective and
totally Spanish. The interjection of the cries and songs of the
street singers, not only here but at several points later in the

opera, is not only notable in the context but looks forward to their more extended and imaginative use in *El retablo*. The two sets of dances and the beautiful Intermezzo which magically conjures up the stillness of a hot southern night and its perfumed languor also have their transformations and transubstantiations in the later works.

That Falla should have lavished his most devoted care and utmost skill on the backcloth of *La vida breve*, and that he should have achieved there his most memorable effects and most original music, rather than in the formal operatic sections, was only to be expected at the time and in the circumstances. If we follow his development as a composer from beginning to end, we shall see at once that his creative powers were invariably released by the historical and spiritual background against which the Spanish consciousness has over the centuries emerged, and that this tends to reveal itself in general rather than particular directions. Falla's music is by no means impersonal, let alone depersonalized, in any narrow or limiting sense. The fierce pride, the aristocratic independence of mind and inward passion of the essential Spanish temperament are characteristic also of Manuel de Falla. Indeed, both in his achievements and his limitations as man and artist, Falla is the most complete representative of the Spanish mind and spirit in music. His compositions are intensely personal (though they are certainly not egocentric after the woollier Romantic manner); but the values are spiritual rather than humanistic: they are not concerned primarily with the doings of the workaday world except in so far as those doings represent universal and specific values. It is thus with *La vida breve*. The simplicities of the 'plot' are in the end overridden by the totality of the creative force that went into the whole conception and its execution which, while it was unquestionably immature, was no less unquestionably authentic in feeling and intention.

There remain several misunderstandings about this opera; and the most curious is the way the protagonist, Salud, is often taken for a gypsy and is still so described in a number of reference books. But this is a clear case of mistaken identity. Falla himself was insistent that Salud is Andalucían, a typification of the southern Spanish woman. The relationship between the gypsies and the true Andalucíans is subtle and often confusing: Andalucíans themselves do not always seem quite clear about it. It is necessary, however, to mark the difference here because Falla was not concerned with gypsy mind and character, as he was subsequently to be in *El amor brujo*, but with something else, something linked to it maybe but still separate and apart from it. He did not even realize that Salud would be taken for a gypsy until it was brought to his notice. He then forcibly opposed the contention. The true nature of Salud was perfectly clear in his own mind, however much it may have been misrepresented subsequently by inattentive criticism and careless analysis.

Despite its immaturities, *La vida breve* made a positive contribution to the emergence of a rejuvenated Spanish national music. Although Falla's touch with dramatic declamation was insecure, his melodic invention still derivative, taken as a whole his achievement in this, his declared opening gambit, was by no means negligible. In the matter of declamation, and of its corollary the reproduction in instrumental terms of the precise inflexions of the language, he was trying to do what Verdi has suggested in *Falstaff*, what Mussorgsky and Borodin had attempted in Russia, and perhaps most pertinent of all what Janáček was doing in and for Moravia. Unlike Janáček, Falla was not specifically interested in instrumental onomatopoeia; but in more general terms and as a parallel to Janáček's way with sound and language, Falla was seeking an absolutely truthful and absolutely authentic style of Spanish melody and declamation, the curve and graph of the musical notation an exact equivalence to the curve and graph of the language. Not until *El retablo* was he to show how far he was able to go in the matter of Spanish declamation and Spanish melodic shaping and shading; but in *La vida breve* he made a necessary start, one that clearly pointed the direction for his later stylistic and spiritual development.

La vida breve was composed in 1904. It won first prize in the competition for which it was written, organized by the Real Academia de Belles Artes. But although one of the undertakings of the organizing committee was that the winning opera should be produced at the Teatro Real in Madrid, *La vida breve* was not performed until eight years later, and then only in a French translation in Nice. Subsequently it was given in Paris; but not until 1914 was it heard in Madrid.

Originally, according to the terms of the competition, *La vida breve* was in one Act; but it was later expanded into two in the interests of theatrical convenience, and it has remained in its two-Act form. Towards the end of his life Falla had it in mind to restore the original one-Act version, but as with so many projected ideas it never materialized.

Although the backcloth and atmosphere of *La vida breve* are localized and pinpointed, the musical style, while in complete harmony with the setting, at the same time reaches tentatively out towards that universality, that conjunction with the main flow of European music which it was Falla's lifelong ambition to achieve. It is not yet strong and imperative; but at least it knows and has declared its direction and makes a positive gesture on the side of freeing Spanish music from the merely local and domestic as represented by the world of the *zarzuela*, from the folk and into the truly national.

The popular *zarzuela* matured in the last decade of the nineteenth century; yet its historical locality, its depiction of customs and scenery belong more closely to the eighteenth, to, precisely, the world known and immortalized by Goya. The influence of Goya on Spanish music, as on virtually all Spanish life and art, is incalculable: the Goya/Scarlatti hegemony tended to dominate either implicitly or explicitly the popular as well as the art music of Spain, the interaction all but beyond clean analysis, deriving from one, informing the other, and *vice versa*.

This is readily demonstrated in the work of the most talented of Falla's colleagues, Enrique Granados, whose piano suite and opera on the Goya theme, *Goyescas*, is pure eighteenth century distilled in terms of the nineteenth and composed in the twentieth. On the other hand, Granados, like Albéniz at his best as well as Falla, could fine down the more obvious clichés of nineteenth-century romantic harmony to something harder, more earthy, nearer to the Spanish bone and muscle, the linear effects of the guitar, via Scarlatti, frequently in the background. This is best observed in the *Tonadillas* for voice and piano where the keyboard parts are almost as original as those in Falla's *Seven Popular Spanish Songs* and like them suffer grievous hurt when orchestrated or otherwise transcribed.

Granados wrote much piano music, a good deal of it in a pleasant but insubstantial cosmopolitan salon style.* He also wrote five operas, of which only one is heard outside Spain. That one, *Goyescas*, has a curious and at the end sad history. First came the set of piano pieces of the same name; subsequently Granados turned them into an opera, with a text by Fernando Periquet who had the difficult task of fitting words to already existent music, a reversal of the more customary procedure. *Goyescas*, in both forms, bids upon the side of that universality and international recognition which was the ultimate objective of all of this generation of Spanish composers—a style based upon Spanish idioms allied to a melodic structure derived from Chopin's *cantilena* and its associated harmonies, together with a Lisztian virtuosity of technique, informed by the rhythms and accents of Spanish dance forms. This process is also apparent in the twelve *Danzas españolas* for piano, a compendium in its way of Granados's piano style and achievement. The curse of Spanish music, especially Spanish piano music, is less its tendency to rhythmic and harmonic monotony due to an over-dependence on regional folk song and dance, than to a surfeit of notes. Over-elaboration and an excess of the purely decorative bogs much Spanish music down in triviality: it has an apparently incurable habit of making mountains out of molehills. This is also true of a certain species of English music, though from a somewhat different angle. Even Falla did not always avoid it, though taken overall Falla's music is remarkable, absolutely as well as relatively, for its economy and precision. But there is often a soft underbelly to Granados's compositions, an emotional and colouristic fulsomeness invariably absent in Falla, even at his most sensuous. Granados's poetic sensibility was genuine and distinct, and he had the typical Spanish pride. All the same, he lacked the hard intellectual idealism verging on arrogance of the great Spaniards. His contribution

* See note 1

was distinguished but limited, partly because of too little dedicated self-discipline.

But, and this is the sad part of the history of the operatic *Goyescas*, Granados's life was cut short by the First World War. He had gone to New York to supervise the production of his opera at the Metropolitan in 1916. He had booked a passage home, but was called to play at the White House before he left the United States. This necessitated him taking a later ship, one bound for England. On 24 March that ship, the *Sussex*, was torpedoed by a U-boat in the English Channel, and Granados, though safe himself, perished in an attempt to save his wife. By a further tragic irony, the *Sussex* did not sink and was subsequently brought to port.

It is impossible to assess the true extent of the deprivation suffered by emergent Spanish music by the death at the age of 49 of Enrique Granados. It is clear that his talent was still not fully matured or developed, even more clear that he still had much to contribute. As it stands, his legacy is *Goyescas*, in both its forms. The opera is a delight, and like the piano suite goes some way towards defining a truly national style of Spanish music. It is at bottom a superior *zarzuela grande*, and the association with Goya reinforces that impression. This is in no way to denigrate *Goyescas*, simply to point a direction and a line of evolution. Like *La vida breve* its dénouement is tragic; but there is comedy in it too, and satire: it opens with that traditionally Spanish custom of blanket tossing known as El Pelele (The Strawman), which is a form of popular entertainment and at the same time a gesture of irreverence towards authority. In this, as in everything else, *Goyescas* is quite unlike Falla's opera, which is without comedy and has no connection at all with the *zarzuela*. *Goyescas* is in fact the more finished composition, the outcome of a more complete and sophisticated technique than *La vida breve*, though its style is generally more 'closed', less fertile for future evolutions.

Before Falla had reached full maturity or Granados embarked upon his fatal sea voyage, Isaac Albéniz had died, in 1909, and at the same early age as Granados. Albéniz, unlike his two colleagues, was enormously prolific, his opus numbers rivalling those of Johann Strauss. He composed many operas, some of them to English texts, and a large quantity of piano music. He was not a particularly profound or original composer, at least not until the end of his life when, between 1906 and 1909, he wrote the two books of piano pieces known collectively as *Iberia*. Here Albéniz caught the true note and temper of Spain, of Andalucía principally. Albéniz was not Andalucían but Catalan, and he approached the Andalucían flavour more objectively than many, leaving out the 'mystique' which has proved a fatal snare for lesser composers, especially non-Spanish ones. The clacks and stamps and clicks so beloved of the purveyors of that bogus Spaniosity which has had such a disastrous effect on the reputation of Spanish music and so obstructed acceptance of the genuine variety, these and all other 'Spanish effects' are not eschewed but assimilated by Albéniz into an original and creative idiom in *Iberia*. Echoes of the guitar, the long cry in the night of the *cante jondo* singer, the rhythm of the dance, the tangible, almost tactile sense of hot sun on parched earth, the breeze off the sea, so obvious on the surface yet so difficult to render unobvious, inform this music without distorting it by an excess of the trite and the commonplace. Maybe there is at times still some legacy of that surfeit of notes that is the bugbear of Spanish piano music; but overall there is a concision of thought and a clearly defined underlying emotion rare in music of this description. The fundamental texture is harder than in Granados, only yielding in these respects to the Falla of *Fantasía baetica*.

Before *Iberia* Albéniz had composed in the conventional salon style, his piano pieces excellently turned but of no real distinction. In some ways the best of them resemble *zarzuelas* in miniature, witty, characterful, totally Spanish in the local and domestic sense, the less good somewhat flaccid and innocuous. But *Iberia* extended beyond narrow limits and so set Albéniz high in honour among those who gave to the outside world a true vision or image of the inner pride and absorption of the southern Spanish nation.

A number of misconceptions about Falla and Spanish national music in general have arisen from want of a proper understanding of both the underlying musical ideals and of the Spanish mind and spirit. Constant Lambert, a brilliant, witty and immensely perceptive critic, missed the point in relation to Spanish nationalism and perpetrated one of the typical misconceptions when he wrote in *Music Ho!* that Falla, after continuing in the Albéniz tradition in a somewhat desiccated manner, only found escape from the obvious cul-de-sac represented by the superficial and picturesque elements in Spanish music by grafting onto his national style a chilly neo-classicism. This is wrong from the start; a basic misunderstanding of all that Falla himself stood for and no less of all that the entire movement towards a Spanish musical renaissance stemming from Pedrell proposed. Falla only continued in the 'Albéniz tradition' in so far as the very best elements in *Iberia* are concerned, and only to a certain extent there. He admired Albéniz and was his friend until the latter's death. But, unlike Albéniz, and for the most part Granados, Falla's music is not essentially picturesque. It has its picturesque elements, naturally; but they are incidental—almost coincidental. It is fair to call Albéniz, as it is fair to call Granados and the less-gifted Turina, pictorial composers in the national idioms of Spain; but it is totally wrong so to speak of Manuel de Falla. At no time or period in his life, early or late, did Falla rely upon mere pictorialism. No man was ever less a purveyor of musical picture postcards.

The definition of Falla's later style as a 'grafting on of a chilly neo-classicism' is also inaccurate and unperceptive. The later style of Falla, his 'Castilian' style, is a natural and inevitable development of his earlier style. It derives from his lifelong dedication to the ideal of evolving a universal musical style out of the totality of the Spanish heritage; not from some aspect of it, the Andalucían principally, but a compendium of all that goes into the making of the regional and emotional varieties that form the Spanish nation *in toto*. This is easily demonstrated by reference to Falla's actual compositions. If we place *El retablo de Maese Pedro* and the Concerto for Harpsichord beside *El amor brujo* and *Nights in the Gardens of Spain,* a clear and satisfying process of natural growth is evident. The 'classicism' of the later works has its origins in the 'romanticism' of the earlier ones, although in this context the loose terms 'classicism' and 'romanticism' have little relevance and apply with even less precision than usual. The mature Falla did not 'react' against the young Falla: each work was another step along the road that was quite consciously and deliberately taken at the outset. The popular elements are no less present in the later works: they are simply transformed and more completely integrated into the creative process at the root. The later works are thus more completely and comprehensively Spanish.

Lambert's analysis of the Spanish contribution to musical nationalism is interesting because it represents precisely that attitude against which Falla's own life was a continual struggle and to the overwhelming of which his energies were dedicated. To assert, as Lambert did, that the Spanish national style was invented by a Russian, Glinka, and destroyed by an Englishman, Lord Berners, is an extraordinary statement. And yet, in so far as it was true, or even suggestible at all, it is a singular reflection on those Spanish musicians whose work and reputations lent substance to the argument in the first place. Falla, whichever way you look at him, is not one of them, although but for him that charge might have been nearer the mark. All that Glinka did was to inaugurate that superficial pseudo-Spanish type of composition, that 'bogus Spaniosity' as I have named it, the tiresome persistence of which is still too often mistaken as genuine but which has nothing whatever to do with the true and authentic Spanish musical tradition that stimulated Falla to his life's work. And in fact any national idiom can be parodied by clever exaggeration and the nailing of salient detail, but no genuine national style can be destroyed by it. The outer trappings of Spanish music are as easy to imitate or parody as the trappings of jazz; and in either case the result is invariably shallow and commonplace.

The Spaniards, Lambert further argued, can show no *Boris*, no *Prince Igor*, no *Coq d'Or*. True; but they can at least show an *Amor brujo*, a *Three Cornered Hat*, a *Retablo*, a *Goyescas* and an *Iberia*; even, despite acknowledged immaturities, a *La vida breve*. It is not necessary to argue out of hand that these Spanish works are comparable in scope and power and magnitude to the great Russian masterpieces. Certainly they are a good deal smaller. But they are no less distinguished examples of a national music that breaks through the narrow nationalistic barriers. In any case, to back the best of Falla against the best of Rimsky-Korsakov is to lose no hostage to fortune, if it comes to that. The comparison is not entirely apt; yet it has been made and is perhaps relevant in a broader context, countering a piece of inadmissable evidence.

The bias, therefore, is not always what it seems; the strands are more complex than they appear on the surface. The links between *zarzuela* and *tonadilla* and the fully fledged national style remain in spite of the efforts of various Spanish composers to disallow and disavow them, no less than with the re-garnered harvest of the far past and the popular elements, notably flamenco, outside the theatre and away from the urban centres. And it is in the life and work of Manuel de Falla in particular that these links and strands come together, the whole woven into a complex but lucid pattern.

III

FALLA: THE FRUITFUL YEARS

ALTHOUGH HE LIVED for 70 years, the list of Falla's published compositions could be written on a single sheet of note
paper; and his known unpublished works occupy even less
space.* Yet, limited though his output was, each of Falla's
major scores is a striking and individual contribution to
twentieth-century music, and each marked an important
advance in his own artistic evolution. No man allowed less
trivia to see daylight under his name. A ruthless self-criticism
and a temperament of the utmost fastidiousness combined
to make Manuel de Falla at once the least prolific and the
most consistent of leading composers. Unlike, say, Edward
Elgar, Falla despised popularity and had no desire whatever
for worldly honours. He possessed neither the inclination nor
the innate ability to compose music that reaches direct to
the hearts of ordinary non-musical people and stirs them
to feelings of national pride and well-being, as both Elgar
and Sibelius not only did but were proud to do. Among
the consciously, even at times self-consciously national composers, Falla was the last to appeal to the patriotic muse to
deliver his message. That does not make him either a greater
or a lesser artist, only a different one.

Falla's reticence and fastidiousness were not external and
deliberately cultivated; certainly in no sense a pose or attitude;
they were a profound and integral part of his temperament
and his innermost nature. Without them he would have been
a totally different man and artist, a human being of an
absolutely dissimilar constitution. It may be argued that what
amounts to an obsession with good taste and the minutiae
of perfection most often signifies some quality of genius in
a way inhibited and less than completely masterful; and it

* See Appendix I

has to be admitted that, judged by the very highest standards, Falla in this respect is found wanting. As he grew older, he became more and more punctilious. After the creative burst following his return to Madrid at the outbreak of the First World War, he wrote only two more major works, discounting the large scale oratorio-cantata upon which he was intermittently working over the last twenty years of his life. It is all very frustrating. If only, one feels, Falla could have more readily and more consistently let himself go, have risked at least a potential bursting of the creative buttons; if only the restraining imp of self-doubt and a critical sense of quite extraordinary severity and austerity had not so often stayed his hand just when the creative process was beginning to warm up ... If only. But the fastidiousness of his private life was exactly reflected in his creative work—and *vice versa*. He was incapable of composing with a kind of reckless gusto, just as he was incapable of living in any but the most rigid and formal manner. He had fire in his belly all right; but even in his earlier and most familiar works, his Andalucían masterpieces, he was reluctant to let it flare and blaze with total freedom.

We have it on the evidence of his friend and biographer, Jaime Pahissa, that, especially towards the end of his life, Falla could not bear to appear in public wearing the wrong boots or a shirt less than impeccably pressed and laundered, or to have his meals served at any but the precise time indicated by his strict personal routine. And just as he shaved each day with the utmost care and thoroughness, so he also tended to pare and polish his compositions down to the last semi-quaver, the ultimate eighth-note. His music seems only to have come forth at all by some force of extreme compulsion, its publication a kind of reluctant necessity. It was not that he didn't wish to compose and publish; his life's aim and ambition was to evolve a truly Spanish national music and send it out into the world to join the mainstream of European music in his day and age, and to remain there for all time. Yet the impression still remains that the labour of birth was for him heavy and arduous and that only stern necessity enabled it to be accomplished. There was probably a good deal more

music than ever appeared that was polished and 'perfected'
into oblivion, if not actually stifled at birth. And maybe
Falla did just that, stifle; or else manage to cover his tracks
so skilfully that he makes Brahms, usually regarded as pretty
apt in these matters, appear a veritable tyro. Either way,
not a note of it exists, or ever has existed.

It is of course an impertinence of criticism to take exception
to any artist for being what he is instead of what we would
wish him to be. We are obliged always to look at the creative
faculty by direct and not by reflected or deliberately angled
light. We have, in short, to accept it on its own terms or not
at all. Falla's fastidiousness was, I must repeat, an essential
part of his genius. We have to understand it before we can
analyse it and so come to a proper assessment of its value.
We benefit neither it nor ourselves by wishing or expecting
it to be something other than it by its own nature is, or by
imposing upon it some private predilection or prejudice.

And in truth, we should not wish Falla's music to be
other than it is. A prolific and uninhibited Falla would be
an irrelevant contradiction, running altogether against the
grain not only of his own genius but in a specific sense of the
spirit and inner nature of Spain itself. All the same, it is
difficult sometimes not to see his extreme fastidiousness as a
form of self-denial which in the end impeded the free working
of his exceptional talent. When he became inspired by a
project and had thoroughly launched himself into it, no man
worked with more purpose, energy and enthusiasm. But as
one reads through his biography, one feels that often a good
honest blaze might have been worked up if only it had been
given a trace more encouragement, if only the gambit had been
accepted, even at some potential risk. But risks of this sort Falla
was constitutionally incapable of taking. He had to be sure,
to search inwardly until every doubt was at rest, every possible
flaw exposed, every contingency examined and allowed for.

A strong sense of frustration pervades Falla's biography.
Even when a work appeared to have reached completion,
it had to be revised and re-polished over and over. He needed
to wait upon inspiration, and inspiration did not visit him
often or easily. And when it did come, he did not always seem

Manuel de Falla as a boy: Cadiz, 1890

'Retrato de Falla' by Vasquez Diaz

Manuel de Falla in middle life

Above : Enrique Granados, from the drawing by Bernadino de Pantorban

Left : Isaac Albéniz

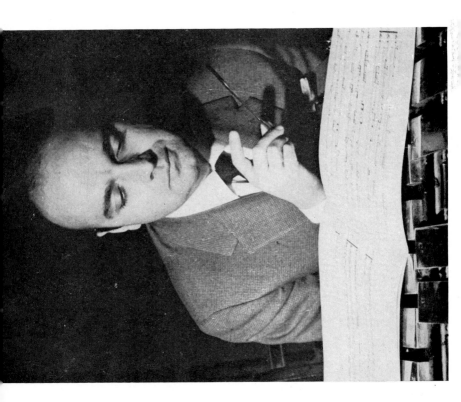

Above : Jesús Guridi

Left : Luis de Pablo

Joaquín Rodrigo with his wife

Left : Joaquín Turina; *above :* María del Carmen de Falla as a young woman; *below from left to right :* Francisco Garcia Lorca; Antonio Luna; María del Carmen de Falla; Federico Garcia Lorca; Wanda Landowska; Manuel de Falla: Granada, *c.* 1927

Manuel de Falla in old age

ready to trust it. Much harder labour and profound searching of heart and mind were necessary before he could realize the music that was in him; and he would rather deny his creative talent altogether than allow anything to appear in public that did not pass the intense scrutiny of that severest of censors lodged inside him. Not, apparently, even then, inevitably. The wonder is not that Falla composed and published so little music, but that he managed to persuade himself to publish any at all. An exaggeration of course: his lot was a hard one; but he had to bear and accept it in order to remain true to himself.

This fastidiousness can be discerned in virtually every work by Falla. Like that other fastidious and ultra-sophisticated composer, Maurice Ravel, Falla was in the habit of making a little music do a lot of work. He did not follow Ravel's practice of frequently orchestrating his piano pieces (or making piano versions of orchestral works) as a means of bolstering his output and making the most of any inspiration of which he was the grateful recipient. Indeed, Falla's music was for the most part conceived so completely in terms of its original instrumentation and physical constitution that few composers suffer more from the attentions of arrangers and transcribers. He has not of course escaped such attentions, but in virtually every case the transcriptions have resulted in a degradation of the original to a greater or lesser extent. Even those who should have known better have been guilty. Ernesto Halffter was a pupil and close associate of Falla, yet he orchestrated the piano parts of the *Seven Popular Spanish Songs* with predictably ineffectual results. The piano version of the 'Ritual Fire Dance' from *El amor brujo* was played by Artur Rubinstein with much panache and has been so rendered by other and usually lesser piano players: it was even arranged for dance band and played by the Ambrose Orchestra in the 1930s (and not badly either); but then it is one of the few purely 'effects' pieces in Falla and so takes more kindly to such treatments. But in general the best one can say about these arrangements and transcriptions is that they are sometimes picturesque and add some note of mild exoticism which appeals to those who think of Spanish music only in such terms.

Falla, of course, expressly disliked hearing his music described as 'picturesque'.*

Falla's habit of making the minimum amount of music do the maximum amount of work can be traced internally even more than externally. In how many of his best and most characteristic compositions do we find small figures and motifs and phrases, even at times whole sentences, used time and again in one form or another, subtly varied no doubt but remaining substantially the same for all that? And the process can be seen at work both in different compositions and within the same one. It is present in works as separated in time and apart in style as *El amor brujo* and *El retablo de Maese Pedro*, and internally within the three movements of the *Nights in the Gardens of Spain*. It also appears elsewhere; so often in fact that it must be accounted a leading principle in the style and structure of Falla's music. Some people have been known to find it so disconcerting that it undermines almost all their potential enjoyment of Falla. They do not carry the day; but their point of view has to be noted as part of the act of disinterested criticism.

The late Ernest Newman liked to remind us that every composer reveals certain basic formulae and structural procedures personal to himself and which lie at the very heart of his creative process. These formulae and procedures are their composers' 'finger prints', and they are not only evident but essential to a genuinely individual style and idiom. Falla has them too, and they are not difficult to track down and enumerate. But that is not quite what I have in mind at the moment. Newman argued that any composer 'when he is in a certain mood or wishes to produce a certain effect he is found unconsciously turning to the melodic and rhythmic formulae that, for him, is inseparably associated with that mood or effect'.† This indeed is the basis of that 'physiology' of criticism upon the value of which Newman laid much stress. It may be verified by reference to the works of every significant composer, and a fair number of minor ones too. Beethoven, Brahms, Wagner; Bach, Handel; Debussy, Stravinsky, Bartók

* See note 2
† *From the World of Music* (John Calder, London, 1962)

—all these spring at once to mind; but the list extends itself almost indefinitely without the necessity for any form of complex inquisition. The late Deryck Cooke devoted most of his invaluable book *The Language of Music*, published in 1959,* to a similar kind of argument and demonstration over an extended field and in detailed instances.

With Falla, however, the position is somewhat different. What one notices here are not only the normal and recognizable 'finger prints', but also a tendency to resort to similar melodic and rhythmic formulae in relation to different moods and in order to produce dissimilar effects. It is primarily in this that the mind of Falla can be seen unconsciously rebelling against the necessity for discovering a large number of new and varied formulae. Falla's music has its own individual stamp: there is no doubt about that. Indeed, there is little modern music that is more immediately recognizable and which expresses a more distinctive musical personality. The 'finger prints' are strong and clear. But, and this is where the distinction becomes important, alongside these are repetitions of formulae and, as they tend to become, mannerisms, which indicate some inhibition in the composer's creative vitality. An analysis of Falla's works shows that there are, generally speaking, fewer basic motifs than there are different moods and feelings. Hence a tendency to overwork such as do appear.

I doubt if the process was in fact entirely unconscious: Falla's method of composing tended automatically towards it, or something analagous. His structural and formal principles were as individual as his harmonic system. But it was his invariable practice to derive his second and subsequent ideas from his initial theme. It was the initial theme that mattered: it wasn't exactly a 'germ', but it was the prime mover and protagonist of the entire composition. In this he frequently resembles Haydn. Haydn also tended to derive his second subjects from his first, and he often made the first subject only mildly varied do duty for both. No one will accuse Haydn of lack of fecundity or any hint of creative inhibition; but it is likely that he did not come by memorable or

* Oxford University Press, London

fructifying themes as readily as most composers noted for great productivity. Haydn's true fecundity reveals itself in his developments. And it is precisely here that Falla differs. Falla was not a great developer. After the initial idea had worked itself through, he was more concerned with detail and with the subtlest effects of colour and poetic evocation. His thematic combinations invariably reinforce the primacy of the main theme. Given Falla's temperament and artistic faculty, anything in the nature of symphonic development was more or less out of the question, and he never attempted it.

Structurally, Falla's music is very simple. That it is also uniquely effective is due to his impeccable sense, partly innate and partly acquired from his studies with Pedrell, of an exact balance between form and content and an absolute certainty of artistic aim. He never, once he was set upon his course after the completion of *La vida breve*, miscalculated. He was far too sensitive an artist ever to begin from fundamentally false premises; or if he did he extinguished it well before it ever had a chance to make a tentative bid for life. He had an extraordinarily just idea of what he was doing and of the right way to do it. But he had no faculty for abstract composition on a large scale. As a modern musical perfectionist he may be compared to Ravel; and he possessed an even finer sensibility and an even sharper self-criticism—so much so that at that far point where Ravel would or had to compromise, Falla would not and did not. He paid a heavy price; but it was one he was by the inner nature of his genius obliged, and willing, to pay.

Falla's temperament was that of a mystic. A Franciscan spirit, Salvador de Madariaga called him; and this to some extent set him apart from the age in which he lived. Although he must be seen as essentially a modern composer, in order to understand him fully and to penetrate to the real heart of his nature, to reach the absolute essence of it, it is necessary to relate him back spiritually to the great tradition of Spanish mysticism of the sixteenth century and before, rather than to the emergent twentieth century of his first maturity. With the nineteenth century he had, despite surface appearances and taking into account his conscious nationalism with its concomitant romanticism, very little in common. That note of profound melancholy which is so often heard in his music is far more a religious than an emotional romantic melancholy. The two are not wholly dissociated; but in Falla's case the distinction is a clear one.

In all Falla's music there are powerful images of ecstatic aspiration and profound spiritual suffering. This is so even in works like *The Three Cornered Hat* which seem to have no tragic implications; yet beneath the vigorous physical celebration and the sharp-edged relationships there is the implicit Spanish sense of a tragic destiny and the dignity of death. Falla does not express the individual isolated from and in perpetual conflict with the world, in the typical romantic manner, but voiced instead a constant striving ever outwards from a passionate centre towards some far and eternal consummation. And although he was strongly attracted to Spanish folk music and in his later years worked hard to help preserve it, he was in no sense a nature poet. Nature does not speak in and through Falla's music. Even in the most 'earthy' of his works, it is the human spirit and the collective consciousness, seeking, active and usually suffering that remains the dominant motif. As he grew older, the naturalistic elements receded farther into the background; or rather they became transmuted in his creative imagination and so emerged as subtly implicit instead of vividly explicit.

Stravinsky once said that Falla's nature was 'the most unpityingly religious I have ever known'. And that is the ultimate truth about him; the one central truth around which all else revolves and to which everything in his life and work is related. Therefore Rodolfo Arizaga's question why Falla did not leave a single work of a religious nature is irrelevant. Every one of Falla's works is in the broadest sense a religious composition, an act of religious conviction. For him the division between sacred and secular may have been real enough in external terms, but from the point of view of the innermost spiritual life it does not exist. For Falla, the act of creation itself was a religious manifestation, a celebration of faith. He was incapable of artistic and creative profanity, in life or in work.

Stravinsky also said that Falla seemed totally to lack humour; and this too comes through. Again, despite the rich humour of *The Three Cornered Hat*, ingrained humour is not a quality of Falla's music any more than it was of his life. *The Three Cornered Hat* is in this as in certain other respects an apparent 'sport' among Falla's works, much as *Die Meistersinger* is among Wagner's.

It is sometimes said that Elgar and Delius represent clear-cut opposites. But that impression does not probe very deep. If Delius is the private poet always, Elgar is the public servant only some of the time, and less of it than used to be thought. It is Delius and Falla who stand at true opposites. The development of Falla's life and music shows a continuous movement towards a more refined intellectuality and a more intense spiritual purification. There are times, by no means rare, when Delius and Elgar tramp the woods and hills together, others when they seem to share a private meditation or pensive nostalgia, in as close harmony as ever possible between strongly autonomous individuals. But Falla is never with them, any more than he is with Bartók in contemplating the minutiae of natural life.

Falla's loneliness is the loneliness of the saint and the ascetic in the day-busy world: his music is thus usually obliged to wear a hair shirt. There is seldom anything lush about it. The sensuality of his earlier works is distilled through the acute sensibility of its creator and subjected to a refining process that releases it as objective rather than romantically subjective. Falla could evoke with great poetic skill the languid sensuousness of a hot Spanish night; but he is never involved directly in it on the human plane. He was emotionally and psychologically reticent to the point of austerity. And the irony is that those who value Falla's music most for its obvious 'Spanishness', for, that is, its colour and vivacity, its sharp rhythms and echoes of the national song and dance, do not understand that the more 'intellectual' his style became, the more comprehensively Spanish did it grow in spirit. The austere and intensely individual Concerto for Harpsichord is totally Spanish in a way that makes *La vida breve* and *Nights in the Gardens of Spain* seem only half way so despite their surface colourations, and even though they in their turn tend to make most other Spanish compositions of the early revival appear merely pictorial by comparison. Even *El amor brujo* and *The Three Cornered Hat*, both superior master-pieces, are somehow only semi-interpretations of the totality of Spain. With the partial exception of *The Three Cornered Hat*, which stands mid way between the Andalucían style and the Castilian style in Falla's output, the earlier works, marvellously piquant and evocative though they are, have to be seen as regionally rather than universally Spanish: the concerto and *El retablo* at once strike deeper and spread farther as imaginative interpretations of Spain herself, whole and indivisible. In his search for a synthesis that would comprehend the Spanish consciousness *in toto*, Falla moved steadily away from the vivid local colours and exoticisms of Andalucía.

A mingling of ascetic mysticism with a form of passionate lyricism is altogether characteristic of Spanish art. It can most forcibly be observed in St John of the Cross and Luis de Leon. The lyric elements are frequently marked by powerful images of drama and strong impulses of emotion, as in the music of Victoria which contrasts sharply with the exalted serenity of Palestrina. Falla was devoted to Victoria and in many ways thought of him as a kindred spirit. In the later music of Manuel de Falla the soul of Spain found its most authentic modern expression; at a range of some three-and-a-half centuries Victoria, Morales and their contemporaries found in Falla a completely sympathetic successor. A great gulf in time separates them and him; but in spirit that gulf is bridged.

If we relate Falla's music to the times in which he lived and to the spiritual and national background from which it evolved, we can see at once a number of striking co-relationships. In Spanish art as a whole there is a strong admixture of two seemingly opposing principles, of what may loosely be called Gothic intellectual idealism and Moorish sensuality. The strength of the latter may be held to account to a considerable extent for the asceticism, the intense drive towards self-purification, of many of the great Spaniards throughout history. Conscious of the danger of over-sensuality, they have tended to veer, with their fierce pride and their incomparable view of themselves as human beings called to the highest destiny, towards the opposite extreme. The Gothic element, in one form or another and upon whatever ground or assumption, is never far from Spanish art at its most potent and most powerful. The more picturesque and colourful aspects of Spanish music and Spanish art in general as it is accepted by the outside world and which have been most avidly seized upon by foreigners, derives primarily from the sensuous appeal of the Moorish heritage, especially as it exists in Andalucía. The Gothic intellectual tradition is less immediately striking to the superficial glance; it is Castilian rather than Andalucían; but it is no less deeply ingrained. The co-mingling and frequent violence of the opposition of these two principles is responsible for the vitality and the enormous potentiality of the Spanish nation, and sometimes for that strange and unnerving dichotomy that from time to time undermines Spain and has threatened her with spiritual as well as material disintegration. In that dichotomy lies the paradox of Spain.

The music of Falla finds these two opposing principles continually at work. Sensuous charm is remarkable in much of his work; but intellectual idealism, never absent from anything he wrote, at any time or period, gradually gains the upper hand as Falla moved spiritually northwards from Andalucía to Castile. And yet—and this is significant in the context of the music of his time in general—just as Falla never surrendered to sensuality and the over-romantic dream, so his intellectualism never became so dominant that warmth of feeling and a genuine, if constantly refined, lyricism was expurgated and a kind of introspective sterility allowed to take over. He walked that particular tightrope with skill and rare judgement in the artistic ambience of the 1920s. As a consequence, the ear in Falla is never affronted, never denied some natural satisfaction, even when he is at his most uncompromising.

Although Falla's career can be seen as dividing itself into certain natural phases or 'periods', it is more remarkable for a steady, unswerving movement towards the fulfilment of a definable ideal. That ideal was the discovery in Spanish national idioms and Spanish history of a genuinely universal musical style. It was, of course, also the ideal in one form or another of all the Spanish musicians of the renaissance, certainly of all those who had come under the influence of Pedrell. Falla, more than any of the others, understood from the beginning that for the 'national' composer to produce works that could fertilize and be fertilized by the mainstream of European music, it was first necessary to achieve emancipation from nationalism for its own sake. He therefore immersed himself in the heritage of Spain's musical past and in the indigenous folk and popular idioms. In this he was by no means exceptional; it was the uses to which he was eventually to put the results of that immersion which were in every way exceptional.

Despite his great knowledge of and interest in folk music, and although every bar of his music is imbued with a profound Spanishness of mind and spirit, Falla made very little use of folk material as such. Even in the ballets *El amor brujo* and *The Three Cornered Hat*, which sound as though they are full of folk tunes, the themes are nearly all original. Falla takes folk and popular material and transmutes it into something rich and new and in context strange, as every national composer worth hearing does and has done; as Vaughan Williams, Bartók, Janáček did. The same is true of Falla's later works, though in a slightly modified way. The street cries that are such a memorable feature of *El retablo*, and the use of fifteenth-century Castilian popular songs as the 'generative theme', as it has been called, of the harpsichord concerto, are not 'copied from nature': they are certain elements among many which have been passed through the texture of the creative imagination and become in the process an integral part of an ultimately trans-national style. Falla was a highly sophisticated composer. He had none of the simple naivety of the peasant-rooted folk bard.

Much play has been made with Falla's indebtedness to the French Impressionists. Like most young Spanish musicians of the time, Falla went to Paris before the First World War

c*   73

and was there helped and befriended by men who exerted a considerable influence on him, notably Debussy, Ravel and Paul Dukas, as well as his compatriot Albéniz, already installed in the French capital. He arrived in Paris in 1907, thus fulfilling a long-standing ambition, and only left in 1914 because of the outbreak of war. Those seven years were of major importance for him. He in his turn made an impression on the French musical world. The '*petit espagnol tout noir*' as Dukas dubbed him was recognized as a man of quality and true talent. He attended assiduously and learnt much. Debussy in particular taught him by example as much as by precept a great deal that he still needed to know. And Falla, for his part, though he had no great opinion of the numerous French 'Spanish' compositions of the order of *España* by Chabrier, greatly admired and was aware of the authenticity of Debussy's evocations of Spain, notably *Soirée dans Grenade* and *Iberia*. Falla asserted that without knowing Spain Debussy had written better Spanish music than most Spanish composers, and that the native composers ignored or despised the authentic effects of flamenco in particular until Debussy showed how to use them.

All this is true enough; but it leads the way to a dangerous misconception. Even at its best, as with Debussy (who only visited Spain once and that for the purpose of attending a bullfight at San Sebastian) and Ravel (whose mother was Basque), French music is never Spanish music. Bizet's *Carmen* is not Spanish music in any sense: it is French music about Spain. And Debussy himself, in *Iberia*, composed a masterpiece in the Spanish manner; but it remains French music. Falla alone composed true and authentic Spanish music of a comparable quality. The relationship between French and Spanish music is both subtle and misleading. With Russian music there is no real connection or relationship at all. Glinka, and Rimsky-Korsakov wrote pastiche Spanish music; but it has little authentic connection with genuine Spanish music.

Russian music was making an impact on Paris during the years Falla was there; and no doubt he learnt from it. But what he learnt certainly was how not to compose Spanish music by proxy: it was a kind of musical nationalistic exercise that gave him a number of valuable clues, the way, principally, to a newly authentic style of declamation, as I have indicated in the last chapter.

More important was the legacy of the Paris Exposition Universelle of 1889/1890 where French musicians, including Debussy, of the sharpest ears, had had the opportunity to hear not only flamenco but just as important, Balinese gamelin music. Here was the source of a good deal of subsequent evolutions in French music; and some of it undoubtedly rubbed off on the attentive Falla.

Although Falla was the most reticent and fastidious of men and musicians, destined by the very nature of his genius to produce a small number of works of singular perfection of style and execution, the period of the First World War and immediately after was, for him, prolific and fruitful. He had gone to Paris, following in the tradition of Spanish musicians established a century earlier by the ill-fated Arriaga, and had been preceded by Albéniz. During these seven Parisian years he had absorbed much; but creatively they had yielded little. Only two new works were produced and published: the *Cuatro piezas españolas* (Four Spanish Pieces) for piano solo, written in 1906 and first performed by the famous Spanish pianist Ricardo Viñes at the Société Nationale de Musique in March 1909, and the *Trois Mélodies* for voice and piano to words by Théophile Gautier, written in 1909 and premièred by Ada Adiny-Milliet with Falla himself at the piano at the Société Musicale Indépendence towards the end of 1910. The *Cuatro piezas* were all but completed before he left Madrid for Paris, and the *Seven Popular Spanish Songs* and parts of the *Nights in the Gardens of Spain* were begun before he returned to Madrid in 1914.

Both the *Cuatro piezas* and the *Trois Mélodies* show Falla's evolving genius and contain pointers to the future. The *Cuatro piezas*, dedicated to Albéniz, are written with that concision and economy that was to become progressively a feature of Falla's musical style and in piano terms anticipate the mastery of the *Fantasía baetica*, while the *Trois Mélodies* demonstrate a maturing insight into the French style which was to come to an apparent head in *Psyché* but lay behind much of his orchestral and vocal style without in any way damaging his natural, and national, musical personality.

Yet although both these works are far from negligible, they still represent Falla in his 'prentice, or learning stage. His full capabilities are not yet revealed; but the ground is now well prepared, and on his return to Spain he was to begin that most fertile and productive period during which he composed most of the music by which he is best known and remembered.

He brought with him from Paris the *Seven Popular Spanish Songs*, a set both masterful and unusual—unusual because it is the only instance where Falla used folk and popular material virtually intact, masterful in the way the piano part and harmonic underpinning adds something real and valuable to the originals and does not simply decorate or embellish them. But the importance of the *Siete canciones populares españolas* goes farther. It was the first significant work in which Falla began to apply the technique of natural resonance which was to be the foundation stone of all his mature style.

Much of the unique sound of Falla's music derives from this systematic development. As a young man he had found on one of the open-air bookstands of Madrid a secondhand copy of Louis Lucas's *L'Acoustic Naturelle*, a treatise which anticipated in the middle of the nineteenth century many of the harmonic theories of the twentieth. Falla said that this discovery revolutionized his entire conception of harmony. It took him many years to reap the full benefit; but it remains the source of one of the most potent, if by-passed, lines of modern harmonic thinking. Writers on modern music theory have paid too little attention to Falla, perhaps because he wrote so few 'important' compositions but more likely because most commentators do not understand or have not taken the trouble to find out exactly what Falla's theory and practice was. In all the analyses of tonality, atonality, bi-tonality, polytonality, pantonality and all the rest, there is barely a mention of natural resonance. The late Rudolf Reti, in his valuable study *Tonality—Atonality—Pantonality*,* does not even

* Rockcliff, London, 1960

mention the name of Manuel de Falla, and few books that have been published since are much more informative. Reti intimated that the technique of modern Spanish music derives principally from Debussy; and that, so far as it goes, is true. But it does not go far enough. Falla was certainly influenced by Debussy and learnt much from him, as were and did most of his compatriots. For one thing, Debussy represented the Latin sensibility in music as opposed to the Teutonic passion for metaphysics. Also, Debussy's 'impressionist' technique came as a liberating force into a world still dominated by German and Italian musical aesthetics. But Falla did not rest there. Debussy made his own solution, and it was a manifestation of major genius; but Falla, being another musician from another country, had a different task in hand, another road to follow, even though he was helped on his way by the French master. Impressionist technique in the Debussy sense, in so far as for him it was precisely relevant at all (as perhaps in the *Nights in the Gardens of Spain*, but hardly at all in *El amor brujo* and *The Three Cornered Hat*, and still less in *El retablo* and the concerto, though more so in *Psyché*), was a starting point, certainly not an end in itself. Falla did not rest where Debussy first led him: in fact he hardly followed Debussy at all, though he acknowledged his indebtedness. Falla, more significantly, enlarged and enriched harmonic resources by a very simple and very fundamental expedient which he first apprehended from Lucas.

And this is important; so important that some practical explanation is necessary, especially since Falla's exact methods and intentions have frequently been misunderstood.

Briefly, the technique of natural resonance is based upon a recognition of the harmonics of the fundamental tone as the essential notes in the harmony, and of proceeding from this to treating the harmonic as the new fundamental. Given this initial hypothesis, harmonic resources become immediately expanded and carried into another dimension: it is then possible to ring the changes on the harmonic status of the individual notes while remaining within a strictly controlled musical knowledge and logic. What Falla liked to call 'cadence harmonies' and had used in embryonic form in parts of

77

La vida breve, were simply the result of this shifting of emphasis and function from fundamental to harmonic and then from harmonic to fundamental within the series of natural resonance. Falla began to apply this technique quite early in his career; but only in the mature works did he erect it into a complete system. Where it was first used as a more or less incidental device, for particular effects of musical syntax, it later became an established and unswerving principle. In the first instance Falla was not of course entirely original. The old church composers knew a thing or two about natural resonance, and although they did not systemize, or even perhaps fully understand it, they exploited it to considerable effect when writing for brass in cathedrals. And of course, it is upon these principles in their most basic form that brass instruments without valves function. And indeed, natural resonance has always played some definite part in musical construction.

But with the entrenchment of tonality, the firm domination of major and minor, which took charge of European music for two centuries after the time of Bach, and not always to its unquestioned advantage, the relevance of natural harmonics tended to be overlooked. There is no need to dispute the enrichment tonality brought to Western music; but it has to be remembered that the 'tonal' era was only one period and that different means and different potentialities lie either side of it. In the later stages, certain composers for the piano, Liszt and Chopin to begin with, sensed its significance. It informs, more or less unconsciously, many of Scriabin's harmonic experiments, though for most of the time Scriabin was too busy with huge mystical visions to systemize any specific piece of compositional technique. Debussy himself, and even more Ravel, often seemed to write for the piano from this broad standpoint. Richard Strauss too occasionally for the orchestra; but again only incidentally. But it was Louis Lucas who rediscovered and formulated its basic principles and its precise musical significance. It also of course had, and has, much to do with the parallel science of acoustics and so with the design of concert halls and the recording and reproducing equipment, especially at the loudspeaker end. But in music it had to wait for the mature works of Manuel de Falla to become elevated to the status of a systematic theory of composition, an all informing theory as mathematically precise as the theories of Schoenberg.

Falla's methods and theories have not been given more attention by musical writers because the results are frequently mistaken for bi- or polytonality. Falla himself strongly objected to this interpretation. But the illusion has persisted. No doubt there is something of a play on words. An analysis of a late Falla score often does give the initial impression of polytonality. One cannot deny that. But in order properly to understand and assess Falla's musical thinking, it is necessary to take note less of the end appearance than of the process by which the result was achieved. The important point is that if we accept superficial appearances and regard certain passages in Falla as polytonal, then they can be seen only as isolated elements, as particular phenomena existing in their own right but apart from and incidental to the main structure of the musical argument. If, on the other hand, we see them as the result of his personal conception of the principles of natural resonance and the resulting technique he evolved from it, then they immediately fit into the larger plan and emerge as fundamental ingredients in a highly organized system. And since Falla took considerable pains to formulate and systemize in his own mind his theories of harmony and 'cadence', his music, especially his late music, is only to be properly understood if in the first place the methods through which it came into being are themselves thoroughly comprehended.

The first major work Falla wrote after his return to Spain was the ballet *El amor brujo* (usually translated as 'Love, the Magician', but in fact untranslatable and unnecessary to try). The *Seven Songs* had been completed in Paris though they were not publicly performed until Luisa Vela and Falla himself gave them at the Ateneo in Madrid on 14 January 1915. But the ballet was written as soon as he set foot once more in Spain, written in the remarkably brief period of six months, a time so short for this most meticulous worker that some doubted the existence of the score until it was shown and demonstrated. In fact, however, this was only part of the story, for the original version first presented at the Teatro Lara on 2 April 1915, was very different from the work as we now know it. And it was a comparative failure when it first appeared, so much so that it virtually disappeared for a time, in spite of the fine performances by the gypsy singer and dancer Pastora Imperio at whose instigation the ballet was first conceived and whose mother, Rosario la Mejorana, herself a celebrated artist in her day, did much to initiate Falla into the varieties of Andalucían gypsy song and the deep legends of race and heritage.

Thus, unlike *La vida breve*, *El amor brujo* is concerned with gypsy life, custom and background. This is not usually misunderstood; the provenance is too clear: but it is as necessary to keep it in mind as it is to remember that it is definitely not so in the case of *La vida breve*.

The mystical side of Falla informs *El amor brujo* as deeply and irreversibly as his feeling for gypsy popular song and dance. The story of the ballet, (the scenario by Falla's friend, the dramatist Gregorio Martínez Sierra, was based on an authentic legend) had a symbolic meaning for Falla. It tells how a young man courting a beautiful gypsy girl, although his love is returned, is constantly thwarted by the ghost of a former jealous and disreputable lover; and of the stratagem by which the ghost is exorcized and the lovers united. The confronting and overwhelming of the brute forces of unregenerate nature, as represented by the 'ghost' power of the former lover, by resolute human mind and spirit is a typical manifestation of the Spanish mind and consciousness (in another context it lies at the heart of and is the real *raison d'être* for the bullfight). The Spaniards are not susceptible to the romantic mystique of Nature. There is no Spanish Wordsworth, or Jeffries—or Delius. Life in Spain tends to be too near the bone, too much a running fight with a harsh and inhospitable, if magnificent landscape, for that kind of romantic association to appeal. Sibelius is nearer; but opposite: the harshness of the Spanish environment is related to heat and the parched earth, that of Finland with the frozen wastes. It depends whether you believe the world will end in fire or ice. Nature in Spain and Spanish art is hard, relentless, hostile, yet at the same time deeply, even mysteriously woven into the texture of human life. That is why, unlike nature in Sibelius, in Spain it does not 'feel' indifferent, implacable, but is a more positive principle. Yet of the Romantic 'consolations of Nature' there is no trace.

The music of *El amor brujo* is entirely individual and in the true sense original. It grew out of the background and the songs and dances of the Andalucían gypsies, and it has about it for much of the time a strangely primitive quality; or rather, a kind of emotional and spiritual elementalism contained within a highly sophisticated technical and stylistic cask. There is also a frequent oriental flavour, not surprisingly in view of the known and acknowledged oriental derivation of many aspects of flamenco. Indeed, the score of *El amor brujo* might well be seen as a full-scale *cante jondo* for voice and orchestra. This is the real meaning and nature of the work, considered in all its aspects.

The setting is usually stated as being a gypsy camp outside Granada; but there is a certain indecision about this. When Falla settled in Granada he indicated a cave on the Sacro Monte as being the ideal setting for *El amor brujo*. But originally it was set somewhere on the southern Spanish coast near Cadiz. The presence of a form of the Cadiz tango seems to support this contention; and the sub-title of 'El circulo mágico', 'The Fisherman's Tale', indicates the near presence and necessary influence of the sea. While this is not a point of far-reaching importance, it is of interest and requires consideration, if only because Falla was always precise in everything he did and any slackness in the conceptual line suggests that somewhere the indications have been confused. One thing is certain: Falla understood, although he still had not been there, the significant differences between Andalucía and gypsy Andalucía, and composed accordingly. But he didn't use a single traditional tune, Andalucían or gypsy, although he did employ with great skill and understanding several of the rhythms of popular dance. In the matter of thematic material he remained true to his own belief that folk music is of most value to the cultivated musician who does not use authentic folk tunes but comes to 'feel' the spirit and essence of them and that way allows them to inform but not take over his own compositions. In this, as in certain other respects, he resembles Béla Bartók whose music is full of the spirit and essence of Magyar folk music but who only used it directly, apart from a few rare exceptions which must always appear, when making specific arrangements and transcriptions.

El amor brujo requires a comparatively small orchestra —two flutes, oboe, two clarinets, bassoon, two horns, two trumpets, tympani, bells, piano, and a smallish body of strings. In its first version it needed even less and seems to have been so over-simplified, almost penitential, that it detracted from the music's innate character. So Falla, after the first unsuccessful performances, withdrew it and set to work to enrich and expand the orchestration, much to its eventual benefit. At the same time Martínez Sierra recast the scenario into one continuous scene in place of the previous two.

In its final form Falla's mastery is complete and unquestioned. The scoring, despite the enlargement, is always restrained but extraordinarily subtle and effective, now evoking the deep mysteries of the ritual dance, now the sound of gypsy guitars, sometimes the oriental melismas which are one of the legacies of the Moorish occupation, or the tango of Cadiz as in the ravishing tune in 7/8 time of the 'Pantomima'. The potent vocal interjections (they are hardly 'songs' in any formal sense) are an integral part of the score, at the farthest pole from mere colourful appendages to it. The concert suite minus the songs is thus an artistic solecism of destructive magnitude, even if Falla himself did sanction it (after all, Beethoven in the interests of achieving performance sanctioned the most appalling mutilations of his late works, even the changing of the order of movements and the omission of parts in the *Hammerklavier* sonata). The 'concert suite' has become less common and less 'necessary' now that we have acquired a better conscience in observing the composer's intentions, whoever he may be: we are still not blameless, but, among other things, the LP record has helped us to find better musical manners by obviating the need for shifty expedients.

Taken in the round and all through, *El amor brujo* is a remarkably attractive and individual work. It shows great imaginative vitality and great penetration of the life and customs it sets out to depict. That it has not held its place in the ballet theatre is due partly to the incorrigible habit of balletomanes of concocting ballets out of wildly inappropriate music while relegating original masterpieces to regular or intermittent limbo, or ignoring them altogether, and, even more, to the probability that outside Spain there are virtually no dancers capable of doing it anything like justice, and very few inside nowadays.

Four years after *El amor brujo* came another ballet, *The Three Cornered Hat*. The two are separated by the *Nights in the Gardens of Spain* for piano and orchestra. But it is as well to consider the two ballets together because they represent Falla's Andalucían style from two opposing standpoints. In them he achieved a remarkable first synthesis of popular idioms transmuted into sophisticated art music. They are in many ways complementary, both in technique and in content. *El amor brujo* is strongly modal in its harmonic foundations, and this gives it much of its 'archaic' flavour, while *The Three Cornered Hat* is no less strongly diatonic. In a sense these two ballets represent the dark and the light sides of Falla's genius, as *Tristan* and *Meistersinger* represent the dark and the light side of Richard Wagner's. It would no doubt be stretching fancy too far to see *El amor brujo* and *The Three Cornered Hat* as the Spanish *Tristan* and *Meistersinger*; yet fancy, if pressed, is flexible, even elastic, and the analogy in the farther regions is not ridiculous. Certainly they are both smaller, in their way more modest; but in any case Falla was working at a time when grandiose theatrical productions were out of favour and the ballet, notably under the far-ranging influence of Diaghilev's Ballets Russes was 'in'. Indeed, it was Diaghilev who proposed and urged on the project of *The Three Cornered Hat*. In the context of the time Falla's works can be seen to occupy their relative positions in succession to Wagner's.

In other respects, technical and stylistic, however, the correspondence slackens, at any rate so far as *El amor brujo* is concerned. The modalism here does not imply a saturated chromaticism. Far from it, for Falla's mind was seeking a totally divergent path and even in this 'romantic' work was pursuing his ideal of purity of line and independence of rhythm and a style in which the basic harmony and the harmonic clashes arise out of the contours of the melodies themselves, which is more or less the opposite of what is the Wagnerian principle of independent chromaticism in *Tristan*. But that is really by the way: what is to the point is the aesthetic and national context which existentially if not historically or technically sets Falla's two Spanish ballets alongside Wagner's two German operas, differences in scale and dimension notwithstanding.

The mystical, mysterious and modal character of *El amor brujo* set a particular stamp on its music, for it derived from the very heart of the subject matter. *The Three Cornered Hat* offers an entertainment of a very different kind. But both are firmly rooted in the same soil, the southern Spanish, Andalucían soil. Yet the second ballet stretches and reaches farther in the matter of formulating a universal musical style founded upon the Spanish national heritage. And from there it moves on towards being more comprehensively Spanish in the national rather than the narrowly regional sense. It still belongs to what must loosely be called Falla's 'Andalucían' period; but we are nearer to the true heart of Spain.

Again, Falla's orchestral skill is brilliant, scintillating, original. But it is directed to very different ends. The elements of the primitive and the exotic which inform *El amor brujo* are completely absent. So is the note of romantic nostalgia. In their place is an earthy vitalism, a vivid humour, and a rumbustious sense of irreverence and debunking. *The Three Cornered Hat* is not in the least mystical or tragic, and it is symbolic in an entirely different way from its predecessor. It is a kind of rustic comedy; an intensely Spanish comedy, full of private jokes and illusions, many of which cannot be appreciated by anyone unfamiliar at a far more than incidental level with Spanish ways and customs. The use of the jota from Aragón as the Final Dance is only one example among many. Externally it is easy enough to appreciate; but a whole world lies behind it and only emerges in full when one has peeled layer after layer off the Spanish onion, so to say. All the same, it is not a comedy of manners and intrigue, after the manner of the typical *zarzuela*. It is a fair-sized world away from that too.

The humour, like the setting and the overall ambience, is deep-dyed Spanish. The Spaniards have a great sense of humour; but they are not good at laughing at themselves and more than most they do not take kindly to being laughed at. This too is a consequence of the historical perspectives, of their intense sense of human dignity, of the pride of the individual, of the ancient and time-encrusted sense of destiny. It has its dangers: any race or nation, or individual, is endangered if the capacity to laugh at the self is absent or submerged. The ancient Greeks had the capacity to laugh at themselves, but the Romans had not, which is why the Greek civilization appears to be more flexible, more elegant, less morose and less a mixture of moral earnestness and self-indulgence; more completely civilized, that is. The French are always willing to laugh at themselves (within limits) but the Germans only in the most self-conscious and unconvincing manner. And it is virtually certain that the Jewish race has been able to survive its appalling history largely because Jewish jokes by Jews are among the best in the world and at their best when taking on some indelible racial characteristic. And the English are always at their worst, their most Philistine, when the ineradicable Puritanism that lurks always within the body social gets the upper hand and overlays the national humour or exaggerates it in the wrong direction.

The Spaniard and his sense of humour is a man walking a high wire on a windy day. It is all, as I say, bound up with his sense of personal dignity. He can laugh at authority because authority is either an abstraction or an affront. But he cannot really laugh at himself because of the danger of appearing ridiculous and so of undermining that very sense of personal dignity which is absolutely central to his world- and life-view. It is for this reason that the Spaniards, though among the best, the most honourable, the most loyal and courageous people in the world, can also be the most difficult. And if they happen also to be high-born Catholics they can be impossible. Yet that impossibility is worth all the effort to penetrate and tends to make the easy-going and merely charming by comparison somehow insubstantial.

In *The Three Cornered Hat* Falla did not have much difficulty in walking the wire. The situation is too deeply embedded in the Spanish consciousness and the Spanish temperament; and in any case the story is taken from an established Spanish classic. On the other hand, the very circumstances give specific point to the ballet and emphasize rather than diminish the particular Spanish impact.

The three cornered hat is the symbol of authority in Spain; and nothing delights a Spaniard more than the debunking of authority. (The Spaniard's everyday attitude to authority tends to be unnervingly ambivalent: on the one hand a fierce anarchical individualist, on the other he appears to accept authority in the larger sense with a mysterious sub-servience. Perhaps he is at heart so sure of his destiny and his dignity that he really does not care. But that is too facile a solution. It remains a weird paradox; another.)

Whatever of that, Falla's ballet is very properly devoted to making the local representative of law and order look ridiculous; aided of course by the representative himself who is determined to put himself into a ridiculous situation. But it is also something more than that. Basically, it upholds the pride and dignity of the individual, both in the obvious sense and at several deeper levels. It is by no means a simple case of good and evil, which is so easy as not to be worth the trouble. It is more subtle, more complex. The Corregidor, gross and coarse though he is, can hardly be called evil so much as pompous, muddle-headed, lecherous, and stupid —a fairly alarming combination in anyone who wields author-ity over others and by no means uncommon; but hardly satanic. His is the epitome of all blundering, scheming, self-satisfied officialdom. Although he uses his authority, via his Alguacils or Civil Guards, for the purpose of trying to seduce another man's woman (the Miller's Wife, who is not at first all that averse to the exercise, in a general and non-specific way), he is no Scarpia. For one thing, he is not nearly clever enough. No heads are cut off, no one gets a knife between the ribs or faces a firing squad. And the Corregidor himself comes to no particularly bad end. The worst that happens to him is a dousing in the mill stream, much enthusiastic ridicule, and an honest taste of blanket-tossing after the honourable Spanish custom. And because he is not evil, only preposterous, we can feel for him a kind of reluctant sympathy. Like Beckmesser, his stupidity, incompetence and pomposity lead to his undoing. He is laughed out of court, not trampled down in hatred. The chortling bassoon tells us so.

The traditional Spanish faith in individual dignity and personal freedom is vindicated, its traducers ceremoniously and uproariously defeated.

As with *El amor brujo*, *The Three Cornered Hat* did not begin in the form in which we now know it. It very nearly began as an opera. Falla had long cherished the idea of writing a comic opera based on the classic novel by Don Antonio Pedro de Alarcón. He even went so far as to ask Carlos Fernández Shaw for a libretto at the time of *La vida breve*, and as a possible alternative. Subsequently, he appears to have discovered that Alarcón's will expressly forbade the use of his book for operatic purposes, which does not quite explain how Hugo Wolf managed to use it for his own opera, *Der Corregidor*, unless at that time copyright laws on Spanish works only applied or could be enforced within Spain. But Falla did manage to obtain permission to use it for a ballet, and Diaghilev was enthusiastic for the idea.

But things were still not that easy. The First World War was in full spate and Diaghilev's international guns were substantially spiked. So the work was first given in neutral Madrid in the simplified form of a mime, as *El Corregidor y la Molinera*, the traditional name of the story in Spanish folklore, in two tableaux. This took place at the Teatro Eslava on 7 April 1917, with an orchestra of chamber proportions. Later on Diaghilev's difficulties eased and Falla was able to begin work on the extended ballet with full orchestra.

The first performance of the new work was given by the

Ballets Russes at the Alhambra Theatre, London, (under the French title *Le Tricorne*) on 22 July 1919. This time it was a complete triumph, one of the most brilliant creations of the Ballets Russes, a masterpiece of composite theatre art with décor by Picasso, choreography by Massine and Ernest Ansermet conducting Falla's outstanding score.

The Spanish dances in *The Three Cornered Hat*, most notably the fandango, the farruca and the jota, are brilliantly re-created and characterized. Unlike *El amor brujo*, the *Hat* does make some use of actual popular tunes, though they are marvellously translated. Because of the nature of the whole the isolation of the 'dances' into orchestral suites is not harmful in the way that it is with *El amor brujo*. Always it is better to attend to the whole, to savour the incidentals, to hear the Beethoven 'Fate knocking at the door' as the Alguacils come to arrest the Miller on a trumped-up charge, the female voice off-stage, the cuckoo clock; above all the antics of the corregidor as mirthfully outlined by the bassoon, incorrigible and irreplaceable. But the suites of dances, they serve after a fashion: they do not traduce.

More important than all this, however, is the way in which Falla advances his use of the technique of natural resonance: it has not yet been erected into a comprehensive system, but its larger implications are strongly in evidence and give the score a good deal of its particular flavour and harmonic spice. The influence of Domenico Scarlatti is also beginning to come unequivocally into the open in the clear lines, the linear character of the music and its scoring, and the wispy humour rooted in the endemic national idioms.

And they are idioms in the plural. There is a touch of the *leitmotiven* at work here, not unusually or very far reaching, but significant from another viewpoint. The Miller's Wife is from Aragón, therefore her 'tune' is the jota; the Miller himself comes from Murcia and so his motif is derived from the first of the *Seven Popular Spanish Songs*, 'El paño moruno'; the dances keep the immediate action within Andalucía, as much by their treatment as by their fundamental nature. In *The Three Cornered Hat*, or *El sombrero de tres picos*, its meaningful Spanish title, Falla made his first really important step towards freeing his own and with it Spain's national music from the confines of regionalism, highly attractive and aesthetically valid though that had been.

In between the two ballets came the three nocturnes for piano and orchestra known as *Nights in the Gardens of Spain*. This is Falla's most purely beautiful work: it is also one of his weakest. Say that it is the Spanish equivalent of *La Mer* and that is not too far from the mark. Falla's 'impressionism' is not the same as Debussy's, though influenced by it; but the affinities are there and should not be mistaken. The *Nights* affords a striking example of Falla's methods of composition at the time, and also of the dual nature of his artistic temperament, in parallel to that of the Spanish temperament itself. Thematically, the three sections or movements grow out of a single motif heard at the outset; and many of the internal repetitions so noticeable in Falla's work, that tendency to use the same formulae for differing purposes, are to be found here. The germinal theme had a curious history: Falla was surprised to discover that Amadeo Vives had begun a *zarzuela* with precisely the same theme; and at first neither guessed the reason. Then Falla remembered that at the time of composition he and Vives had been living in the same house in Madrid and that in the street below an old blind man used to play an out-of-tune violin and that those 'seed' notes were the ones the old busker used to repeat over and over. It had formed a theme which planted itself in the sub-conscious minds of both Falla and Vives and, as so often happens, turned up when needed to form an apparently original and independent piece of thematic material.

Throughout the *Nights* Falla uses colour in an unusually self-contained manner. Instrumental colour here, and in certain other works as well, is not applied from without but treated as a primary element in composition. If we examine this score in detail we cannot help being struck by the manner in which instrumental colour is used as an integral part of melody and harmony, and at certain times of rhythm also. It is not an additional ingredient used for purposes of embellishment or decoration. It was, in this case at any rate, perhaps Falla's substitute for the invention of a variety of melodic formulae and in a sense one of his unmistakable 'finger prints'. Falla, whose ear was one of the most acute known to modern music, seldom orchestrated more sensitively or with more poetic relevance than here. The *evocación* is unparalleled: the danger is that it may take the place of true musical substance.

From the aesthetic point of view *Nights in the Gardens of Spain* reveals very clearly from a particular standpoint the dualism inherent in the Spanish temperament and consciousness and therefore in Spanish art. The score contains as perhaps no other does, at least as directly, and with the utmost subtlety, the twin poles of Moorish charm and sensuality and Gothic intellectual idealism. The floating arabesques, the nocturnal warmth and emotive poetry complement perfectly the beautiful architecture of the Alhambra, with its gardens and fountains and cypress trees, the supreme legacy in southern Spain of the Moorish occupation. Yet underlying this there is an outline of strong, lean rhythmic structure; the crisp accents and occasional asperities of harmony and texture pay their tribute to the great tradition of the Spanish Gothic. The sweet-melancholy strains in the hot summer night contrast sharply with the hard bite of spiritual aspiration and idealism, implied rather than explicit but active none the less. If the charm and sensuality are the most immediately striking elements in the seductive 'Symphonic impressions' as the sub-title on the score has it, that is because of its poetic origins in the mind of the composer, origins that go back to Paris where the embryonic idea first came to him. At first he intended some nocturnes for solo piano; but first Albéniz and then Ricardo Viñes moved in with advice and suggestions, and ultimately the idea for piano with orchestra came through. Obviously the original piano nocturnes were of a dreamy and loosely 'impressionistic' nature. The suggestion, from Viñes, who ultimately received the dedication, for the piano-orchestral form released additional energies in Falla. In the event he pocketed the original material and completed the final score at Sitges near Barcelona in 1915. So the Great War years again proved fruitful.

The *Nights*, or *Noches*, is not a virtuoso display piece but a concertante work in which the piano part is integral with that of the orchestra. It has been compared to Vincent d'Indy's *Symphonie sur un chant montagnard français*, but the resemblance is superficial and entirely external—little more than a matter of both works being in the concertante rather than the display category. In both form and intention the two works diverge at virtually every point where it matters. It is in any case unimportant and is only mentioned because the comparison persists in being made.

The weakness of the *Nights* comes from the way the material is expanded beyond its natural limits and, partly because of this, the style is somewhat nebulous. It may be Falla's most beautiful work, but it is also his most indulgent. It is 'impressionism' in the wrong sense for much of the time, the sense that made Debussy speak in sharp disdain of 'an effect of reality, but what some fools call Impressionism, a term that is utterly misapplied especially by critics who don't hesitate to apply it to Turner, the greatest creator of mysterious effects in the whole world of art'. Falla was no doubt also trying to create 'an effect of reality' and 'mysterious effects', but in the *Nights* he tended to let the focus slip and become diffused, not at the edges only but at the centre. The economy and precision of his best work, as of Debussy's (and Debussy was speaking then specifically of his own magnificent orchestral *Images*) is to some extent dissipated by allowing the three parts to become too long for the material, but also because the *evocación* is inclined to undermine the effects of reality.

There is no 'programme' to the *Nights*; it is not intended to be descriptive. It is based upon the 'rhythms, modes, cadences, and ornamental figures which distinguish the popular music of Andalucía', and as always with Falla the use made of such material is authentic and idiomatic. And it is beautiful, yes; there is no doubt that it is beautiful. But neither the form nor the writing for the piano is particularly striking or original, and somewhere at the heart is a softness which sets the music nearer than anything else in Falla, certainly anything on a comparable scale, to the picturesque and decorative music of Albéniz and Granados.

No doubt the *Noches en los jardines de España* (again to restore the dignity of its proper title) was necessary to Falla, an essential emanation of his genius; something that had to come out and served a significant purpose in so doing. And certainly he spent his usual fastidious care on the score. It was given first in Madrid in April 1916, the young José Cubiles playing the solo part, Enrique Fernández Arbós conducting. But by the time it was given in London in 1921, with Falla himself at the piano, it had undergone the usual further polishing and revision.

At one time Falla had intended to incorporate a fourth section, based on the tango of Cadiz; but in the end he used that for *El amor brujo*. The result for the *Nights* was to lay further emphasis on one of its weaker points—the way in which all three sections tend to sound much the same. There is too little variety, especially of tempo. Somehow, somewhere, one has the impression that the score is not perfectly focused because it was not perfectly clear as a total conception in the composer's mind. It may have become so after the event, so to speak, (a fairly familiar process: do it first and explain it afterwards); but it was not really Falla's natural way: certainly one never has a hint of such an impression with either *El amor brujo* or *The Three Cornered Hat*.

Perhaps the slight unease one feels in respect of the *Nights*, and still more the reasons for it, indicate how complex and demanding was the real problem Falla had set himself. The achievement of a universal style based on Spanish national idioms had to be worked towards from several different directions. And it was as much a question of finding out what not to do as discovering exactly what had to be done. The *Nights* would have been hailed as a masterpiece if it had been written by Albéniz or Granados, let alone a minor figure like Turina. From Falla it is still a fine and evocative work, expressive in its poetry and searching in its techniques. But from him it was still not enough. Perhaps one of the things it emphasized was the limitations of all regional idioms, even one as rich as that of Andalucía. *The Three Cornered Hat*, though it is still set in Andalucía, has already moved on in style and the larger national potency. If only the luxuriance and indulgence of the *Nights* could, eventually, be pared down to the concise and economical Concerto for Harpsichord, where there is not a superfluous note and which is built, like the *Nights*, on a single germinating motif; but to reach the harpsichord concerto from the *Nights*, a huge amount of refining needed to be done, imaginative rather than technical: to reach *El retablo* from the *Hat*, however, was another matter. In a number of ways, *The Three Cornered Hat* is the key work in Falla's career; the stylistic pivot between the earlier Andalucían works and the later, consummating, Castilian ones.

IV

A UNIVERSAL STYLE

IF *The Three Cornered Hat* is the pivotal work in Falla's artistic evolution, his next important composition, the *Fantasía baetica* for solo piano, is in a similar sense the link between the earlier 'Andalucían' style and the coming Castilian one with its farther ranging overtones and its consummated move out of the regional and into the universal, the truly international. But this process was neither final nor abrupt, certainly not a cutting off of limbs or a tearing up of roots. On the contrary, it resulted in a strengthening of both, of limbs and roots alike. When Falla turned, artistically, from Andalucía to Castile, from, that is, the periphery of colourful, atmospheric, exotic Spain to the true centre of classical Spanish thought and feeling, it was neither a total reversal of course nor a deliberate rejection of all that had gone before. It was, as a process, additive not subtractive; it was a matter of growth and expansion towards a predestined centre, but in no sense did it imply self-conscious 'reaction'. It was essential inner growth from the smaller to the larger; a complex reaching out towards what had been inherent from the start but had required a somewhat circuitous route before it could reach its destination and find its fulfilment.

To say that there remain elements of the Andalucían style in the succeeding Castilian assumption is to say no more than that Falla's creative faculty was one and unified, not fragmented into separate divisions, compartmentalized so that any one aspect of it must automatically exclude another. Nor is it to imply that the 'purification' was incomplete; that the progress towards a universal style required outright rejection of its regional foundations.

This is well exemplified in the *Fantasía baetica* which, probably more than any other composition by Falla, combines

Andalucían *evocación* with Castilian severity of style. Para-doxically, it is also in certain respects the most prolix of his works: in it he appears to come nearest to that surfeit of notes all too characteristic of Spanish piano music. If, as has been suggested, this is Falla's tribute to Albéniz on the tenth anniversary of the latter's death, that particular aspect of its technical execution and pianistic style would be readily explained. Yet at the deeper level there is a hardness, a purity and inflexibility at its musical and emotional heart that is a clear indication of the direction in which Falla's mind and creative force were moving, migrating as it were north-wards from the sunny south to the heart and kernel of the Spanish consciousness, to the Castilian stronghold.

On the other hand, much of the hardness and harshness of the *Fantasía* is no less rooted in Andalucía, in the often harsh and bitter tone of the *cante jondo,* of the fierce rattle of the flamenco guitar in its aggressive moods, of the stark sense of tragedy and doom that lies in the deeps of the Andalu-cían soul as a vital and integral part of the total soul of Spain. In these as in other respects the *Fantasía baetica* (also spelt *bética*) is as significant a link work in Falla's catalogue on a small scale as *The Three Cornered Hat* is on a larger and more comprehensive canvas. Indeed, the name itself is revealing: *baetica*, or *bética*, was the old Roman name of Andalucía; thus the reference is to the classical world as well as the Spanish south and its specific character. It is an intriguing question just how closely associated in Falla's unconscious these two aspects in their current juxtaposition were before they rose to the surface in the form of a particular composition.

The *Fantasía baetica* thus contains many elements, not all of them apparent to the superficial glance. Falla had in fact, according to Pahissa, conceived the idea for the *Fantasía* during the First World War, when Artur Rubinstein, who was in Madrid at the time and in the process of establishing his world-wide reputation, asked Falla to write a piece for the piano. Rubinstein himself gave the première in New York in 1920 as dedicatee, because he had no time for rehear-sals for the projected first performance in Barcelona; but thereafter he hardly ever played it. And it is beyond question that the *Fantasía* has not generally pleased the legion of virtuoso pianists, at least not to the point of regular performance. In recent years, certainly, it has been recorded several times, and it is currently appreciated by those who know. But during the first decades of its existence it did not make much of a showing. Falla himself appears to have thought that the reason might have been that it was too long and considered shortening it. But fortunately he was soon talked out of that idea. True, the *Fantasía* is a somewhat indeterminate length—too long for a comfortable display piece to round off a programme or use as an encore, too short for a central place in recital. But that is no real reason for perpetuated neglect. More likely is its technical difficulty. It is not, purely in pyrotechnic piano terms, all that difficult; yet its difficulties do not lie easily for the hands, as much of Liszt's virtuoso music does—it certainly doesn't 'play itself' as again the Liszt sonata may be said to 'play itself' if you have mastered basic keyboard technique in the first place. And therefore, the mastering of the *Fantasía* requires the kind of hard work that does not immediately yield quick rewards in public. Why Rubinstein seems to have jettisoned it almost at once is harder to say, for Artur Rubinstein has never been a pianist to seek easy popular acclaim: he has never needed to. Pahissa also asserts that Falla once told Rubinstein he was thinking of arranging the *Fantasía baetica* for piano and orchestra; but that, if it ever was a serious proposition, was one of those sparks that did not ignite, something which frequently happens with artists of all kinds, indeed among workers in virtually every field of activity. The spark flashes but does not leap across the gap.

Ann Livermore* notes many allusions to Albéniz's themes and late piano technique woven into the texture of the *Fantasía*, and from this deduced the act of homage to the older composer and friend whose death in 1909 had affected Falla deeply. It may be so, though no open declaration of that intent was made by Falla himself. In any case, it is not the important factor, which is the innermost character of the music itself. The technical and emotional range is wide,

* See note 3

surprisingly wide perhaps in a work of this nature and this dimension. In the last of the four *Pièces espagnoles* (*Cuatro piezas españolas*), 'Andaluza', written in Paris before 1914, there are the vivid rhythms and melodic melismas of flamenco. And this is the starting point for the *Fantasía baetica*. Here too are the echoes of bittersweet song, the sound of heel and toe, the ecstatic swirl of the dance. But now it is all richer, more complex, more totally integrated, more 'sublimated' as it might be in a certain way of putting it: it is no longer directly representational because it encompasses deeper and more subtle regions of the creative response and imagination.

But that is not all. As well as the added depth and scope of the *Fantasía* there is something else, something that exposes the continuing evolution of Falla's mind, an unmistakable intimation of the next step in the development of its essential character. And this is precisely the foretaste of the Castilian style I have already drawn attention to. It lies deep in the musical style and was no doubt in part unconscious, or if not entirely that then at least a subconscious process at work. We know that in virtually all creative acts, every making of something new and original, there is an unconscious element operating and that it is at least as important and formative as the conscious, the willed and deliberate part of the total act. And this is no less true of artists like Falla (or Stravinsky) where every act is preceded by careful thought, calculation even, as for the more instinctive or 'inspirational' type. The unconscious, both individual and collective, plays a varyingly decisive part in the creative process, whatever the direction it may at any particular time take or whatever the specific content. Thus the *Fantasía baetica* reveals more about Falla's artistic growth at the time when he appeared to be at the point of major change, the point, to put it plain, where his biographers and commentators, and in certain respects himself, see him as abandoning the regional or Andalucían style of his first creative years for a more universal or Castilian style. The difference appears from the outside crucial; and in the context of Falla's own evolution and that of Spanish music as a whole, it is. Yet these 'changes' and apparent alterations of course are seldom as total or as sudden as they may seem on the surface. They are deep rooted, and their presence can usually be felt before they actually happen. At bottom there is, if only in retrospect, an essential continuity without which the creative faculty itself can all too easily fall into disparate sections, become the victim of self-division and so nullify its own best potentialities.

Ironically, the *Fantasía baetica*, usually accepted as Falla's last 'Andalucían' composition, was written at precisely the time when he took up permanent residence in Granada. 1919 was a fateful year for Manuel de Falla: it saw the first success of *The Three Cornered Hat*, the composition of the *Fantasía baetica*, and it also saw the commissioning by the Princesse de Polignac of the puppet opera *El retablo de Maese Pedro*, which was to become one of his finest and most comprehensively Spanish works. Even more than the Concerto for Harpsichord, *El retablo* seems to enshrine the spirit of both modern and historic Spain and to forge a true existential link between them.

But 1919 was no less significant on the personal plane. In that year both his parents died. After his return to Spain from Paris in 1914, Falla lived with his parents in Madrid, visiting other parts of Spain for performances of his works or for professional engagements. But when first his mother and then his father died in the second half of 1919, he was faced with a major domestic upheaval as well as a double private sorrow. He never married or, so far as we know, had an intimate relationship with any woman outside his own family. So after the deaths of his parents he went to live in Granada with his sister, María del Carmen. And this was to set the domestic pattern of his life for the rest of his days. María del Carmen was to be his constant and devoted companion, in Spain and afterwards when he had gone into voluntary exile in the Argentine and there ended his lifespan in 1946, along with his brother Germán, the faithful (and jealous) guardian of his reputation and his artistic legacy.

Falla was much taken with the idea of writing a piece for the Princesse de Polignac's private theatre in Paris. But before he did so he produced another short item that has become one of his best known and most frequently performed works. If it is true that Manuel de Falla wrote some of the best of all guitar music but with one exception regrettably did not write for the guitar, that single exception is enough to clinch the general argument. It is the *Homenaje*, subtitled 'Le Tombeau de Claude Debussy', which he wrote in 1920 following promptings from Miguel Llobet, star pupil of Tarrega and one of the major influences on the pre-Segovia evolution of the Spanish guitar. The occasion was a special issue of the Paris *Revue musicale* to honour Claude Debussy who had died in 1918. The special issue contained articles (Falla contributed one) and a supplement of music entitled 'Tombeau de Claude Debussy' with contributions by most of the leading composers of the day, including Bartók, Stravinsky, Ravel, Satie and Roussel.

Falla's *Homenaje* begins in the rhythm of the habanera and as it proceeds echoes some of Debussy's own music, notably *Iberia*, and towards the end incorporates sombre reminiscences of *Soirée en Granade*. It was the *Soirée* which had so impressed Falla in Paris and prompted him to assert that generally speaking French composers, and Debussy in particular, knew a good deal more about the artistic use of Spanish folk material than most Spaniards did. The whole *Homenaje* was thus a fitting tribute from one master to another, and the incorporation of the *Soirée* reminiscence by no means simply coincidental. The first performance of the piece was given on 2 December 1922, in the Salle du Conservatoire, Paris, by Emil Pujol, another important figure in the modern evolution of the Spanish guitar.

But it remained Falla's sole contribution to the repertoire of the instrument that above all is associated with Spain. A further piece was projected, to be called *La Tertulia**; but as it turned out that was another misfire. Otherwise all Falla's guitar music was written for orchestra or piano, or both together.

Although he was enthusiastic about the Polignac project, Falla was at first at something of a loss for a suitable subject. However, the idea of using the puppet episode from *Don Quixote* suddenly occurred to him, and thereafter it was all

*cf. Pahissa, Appendix II

fairly easy sailing. He made his own libretto, and set to work. He could hardly have chosen better or more appropriately.

Of all Falla's works, *El retablo* is at once the most forward and most backward looking; in other words. it is the most totally and comprehensively Spanish, seeing that the true Spanish temperament is deeply rooted in the glories of the past but at the same time alertly aware of the potentialities of the present, even if, for it, that potential has too often remained largely unrealized. And nowhere is this better exemplified than in the extended use of the harpsichord throughout the score. The harpsichord is an instrument of the past; but it was also, through the artistry and advocacy of Wanda Landowska, returning to favour during the 1920s after centuries of neglect. Landowska was largely responsible both for the return of the harpsichord to its historical importance and for refashioning it and ideas about it as a modern instrument highly suitable for the linear rather than harmonic ideas of the contemporary music of the time. Many modern composers were writing music for her, and Falla became one of them; for the harpsichord part in *El retablo*, directed to be *aussi puissante que possible* indicative of the intention, was first performed by her: no doubt the direction on the score had her forceful style and her strong-toned Pleyel instrument specifically in mind, and was intended to avert any suggestion of the pretty tinklings still to be heard from over-reticent harpsichordists. Neither here nor in the concerto was Falla interested in archaic triflings: he wanted, as in virtually all his music, bold, clearly defined tone and execution.

In other ways too *El retablo* unites the Spanish past and present. It carried to a new and profound synthesis three primary elements—the use of popular street songs and cries, the archaic Romanesque music of the Middle Ages, and the technique of natural resonance—all of which had shown their hand in earlier compositions but which now reveal their fullest inner motivation. In the vocal parts, and especially in the peculiar and unique style of recitative-narration allotted to the Boy (usually delivered by a soprano but properly requiring a treble), Falla at last achieved that totally Spanish declamation he had been tentatively searching for in *La vida breve* and which lay behind the style and contours of much of his intervening music, both vocal and instrumental. This half-speaking, half-singing type of story-telling was once a ubiquitous feature of the streets of the Spanish towns, and can still be heard embryonically in remote villages. Falla certainly heard exponents of it at first hand in Madrid during his youth. It was something entirely Spanish, and if like so much else of true national identity it has more or less disappeared except in the outlying rural areas and will soon vanish there too as television and modern technological amenity moves in, Falla's little puppet show idealizes and preserves it.

In a slightly different way, street cries and street songs, of vendors and hawkers, of watchmen and town criers, were to be heard in most European towns, certainly in London (several of the English composers of the sixteenth and seventeenth centuries wrote elaborate fantasies on them), but they seem to have endured longer in Spain than elsewhere, which again is simply in keeping with the way the old traditional life and customs were preserved there well after the modern technological and industrialized world had imposed its grey uniformity and anonymity in other countries. The street cries and songs of Madrid are closely interwoven into the texture of *El retablo* just as the songs and dances of Andalucía are woven into the textures of the earlier works. One has only to recall the use of such material in *zarzuelas* to recognize how much farther Falla went in this direction as in so many others, and how much more creative his responses to it were. But the line and lineage is the same, even though Falla once again demonstrated decisively how little of the merely picturesque and parochial there is in his mature music.

Outwardly, *El retablo* is quite unlike any of Falla's previous compositions. It is unlike any other Spanish composition for that matter, though perhaps it should not be and would not be if the lead given by Falla had been followed. Yet in the context of Falla's life and work a clear and logical progress within a single creative process is easily discerned. The opening of the music for Melisendra (Scene II—figure 30) obviously grew out of *El amor brujo*. But it is completely in place in *El retablo*, so completely in place that no one can mistake the continuous process that led from one to the other. Falla's singleness of aim and purpose set him early on a road from which he never once deviated. Most composers have, so to say, their extramarital musical flirtations, their relaxations on the back stairs. But not Falla. There were no skeletons in his musical cupboard.

Or perhaps in any other cupboard; certainly not a moral one. Yet looking at Falla's music here for Melisendra one cannot help remarking how sympathetically sensitive his music for his women characters so often is. Salud in *La vida breve*, Candelas in *El amor brujo*, and now Melisendra; even in a slightly different way the Miller's Wife in *The Three Cornered Hat* (though that is but a further slant on the same subject). The contrast between the austere side of Falla as revealed in his daily life and in certain aspects of his music and the passionate nature unleashed in many compositions, especially those from his so-called 'Andalucían' period but lying only just beneath the surface of the 'Castilian' works, purified if you like but never devitalized, is remarkable.

Even more remarkable, though no doubt psychologically linked, is his almost Mozartian sensitivity towards his female characters. How was it that this celibate, ascetic, monkish man could feel the pulse and emotional heartbeats of women in music with so absolute a certainty of touch? It is by no means a common gift. Classical heroines tend to be merely statuesque (exception: Purcell's Dido), while Romantic ones are usually a cross between the sweet maiden and the harridan. Women in Beethoven (also celibate) are invariably cast in the heroic mould, Leonora-like types of formidable character and probably clasping a score of the *Eroica* symphony to their stalwart bosoms. For Brahms (yet again celibate, in principle anyway) women were either whores or angels and often diguised musically by small cryptograms embedded in the bodies of his compositions. Wagner's heroines, even the most indulgent, are always liable to hurl a spear if provoked. Even Verdi's, magnificent as they can be, are frequently, like all Italian operatic women, to be detected in the act of throwing musical tantrums.

But Mozart's feeling for women in his operas is uncanny. They are entirely feminine, women through and through; they are never warriors of the bed or the battlefield; neither milksops nor abandoned temptresses. Women may be any or all of these things at one time or another; but to penetrate the real and essential heart of the female mind and character is a rare, a precious gift which Mozart of all musicians possessed completely. Some, like the late Eric Blom, have suggested that this had its origins in Mozart's personal life, that it was in some way a substitute or compensation for that lack of perfect understanding between himself and any mortal woman which he longed for but never found. Maybe: it has a ring of truth, even though it could be said of more composers than Mozart. But there is no evidence that Falla ever sought that close association and perfect understanding at any time in his life. If, as W. B. Yeats affirmed, lost love is one of the ingedients out of which poetry is made (and that is no magisterially original thought), it does not seem to have been applicable to Manuel de Falla. Yet he too had a markedly close sympathy with and understanding of his women characters of a similar order to Mozart's, if not perhaps to the same degree. It is an intriguing question; and maybe it throws further light into the life and work of this enigmatic and in many respects secretive man.

Another thing: I have spoken before of the close historical correspondence between Spanish and English music; and now it comes again, unexpected almost but not quite inexplicable. For into this most indelibly Spanish of all musical compositions come sudden melodic melismas which, with the hand over the page and the ear unfamiliar with the immediate context, could readily be taken for something by Vaughan Williams. There are hints of it in Melisendra's music, harking back to *El amor brujo* where in 'Escena' (Scène), beginning at nine before 36 oboe and then flute outline a kind of melisma that is complementary rather than similar to the English variety. But in *El retablo* the correspondence is a good deal closer: I think particularly of the passage beginning for solo violin and alternating with viola at eight before 64, which surely might have come out of or gone into parts of *Flos Campi* or Elihu's Dance from *Job*.* It is curious and it fascinates, no more or less because the Falla came first. But the correspondence must have been instinctual: it is certainly unmistakable. Nor can it be laid at the door of contemporary fashions in composing, for this is not at all what was going on in forward musical circles at the time.

By coincidence Stravinsky and Erik Satie were both invited to write a piece for the Princess de Polignac's theatre. Stravinsky replied with *Renard*, Satie with *Socrate*, though neither of these was in fact ever presented at the princess's house: only Falla and *El retablo* had that particular distinction; and even *El retablo* had a first concert performance in Seville —by all accounts not a very polished or successful one— at a private concert of the Sociedad Sevillana de Conciertos. The full presentation in the home of the princess was on 25 June 1923, Landowska at the harpsichord.

Stravinsky's association with the project that led to *El retablo* has another point of interest. In several passages there are clear affinities with Stravinsky's methods in Falla's scoring. I will not call them 'influences' in the direct sense because Falla's autonomous creative personality remains in charge and in any case Stravinskyisms were in the air and could hardly be avoided, especially since they so accurately reflected the current of thought and technique in music during that time. All the same, if we place certain parts of *El retablo* beside certain passages in *Petrouchka*, one or two technical correspondences emerge. I think especially of Scene III, 'El suplico del Moro' (41) and the passage for trumpets and percussion to 44. There is a Moor in *Petrouchka* and there are Moors in *El retablo*. But it goes farther, and deeper, than that: Stravinsky's influence through the 1920s was all-pervasive.

Nor does it end there. The physical dimensions and format of *El retablo*, though ostensibly designed to accommodate the princess's private theatre, were very much in line with the economical and even austere aesthetics of musical production of those days. Partly for economic reasons, partly from a reaction against the magniloquent and the romantically indulgent, musical fashion after the First World War was

*See note 4

all for the small scale, the chamber proportion, the Gargantuan orchestras and huge musico-dramatic sets of the pre-1914 era replaced now by conscious limitation of both ends and means. Stravinsky's *L'Histoire du Soldat* and *Renard*, as well as many of the orchestral and instrumental works of the 'neo-classical' period; the ironic musical commentaries of Satie, much else emanating from France, pointed the new directions. Even Schoenberg, the most prolix of German composers at his outset, laid a stamp upon the new age with music of restraint and physical limitation, leading eventually to the ultimate stylistic economy and 'purity' of Webern. Opulence was out; precision, economy, restraint everywhere. In literature the simplistic prose of Hemingway in place of the subtle complexities of late Henry James. It was not new, of course: it never is. It had already begun in Schoenberg whose Three Little Orchestral Pieces of 1910 pointed the way for Webern's extreme brevity and concentration, 'density' as Schoenberg himself named it. But it went back beyond that, to Mahler, that prime indulger in the giganticism of the late Romantic sunset who would at the same time draw from massive and massed choral/orchestral resources passages of the utmost delicacy and chamber-like definition. Even to Berlioz of whom much the same could be said.

All this—this economy, precision, restraint of both expression and means—suited Falla perfectly. It accorded exactly with his own temperamental bias; and as he grew older the more pronounced did it become. In certain superficial aspects the work nearest to *El retablo* is *L'Histoire du Soldat*. The stage setting, different though in many ways parallel, is only a coincidental point. Nor does nationalism in any significant sense come into the argument, though Stravinsky, the great cosmopolitan of modern music, was in fact as deep-dyed Russian, and acknowledged it, as Falla was Spanish, and in a number of works culminating in the masterpiece *Les Noces* was as tough and hardened a Russian nationalist as any who never left the base. But the neo-classic works of the 1920s and 1930s, though the productions of a profoundly Russian mind and temperament, were not 'nationalistic'. Yet the little comic opera *Mavra*, begun in 1921, is as nationalist as anything in or out of Stravinsky and is actually dedicated 'to the memory of Tchaikovsky, Glinka, and Pushkin'.

The connections, internal and external, between Falla and Stravinsky cannot be pressed too far. Yet they may, as so often, be found illuminating, throwing light both ways, if sometimes obliquely, aiding total comprehension of both composers. And if they illuminate Falla rather more than Stravinsky, that is no doubt because so much more has been said and written about Stravinsky than about Falla, and also because Stravinsky wrote so much more music than Falla, therefore the oyster of the inner man is that much more easily opened, less, inevitably, concealed behind the hard outer shell.

In view of the analogies between Falla and Stravinsky, especially those between *El retablo* and *L'Histoire du Soldat*, and even if, as I have said, they should not be pushed too far, it is worth pursuing the whole matter a stage or two further. In a number of respects, notably those to do with nationality in music, Stravinsky and Falla appear to have thought along very much the same lines.

Apropos of *Mavra*, Stravinsky said that the dedication to Tchaikovsky was also a piece of propaganda:

I wanted to show a different Russia to my non-Russian, especially to my French, colleagues, who were, I considered, saturated with the tourist-office orientalism of the *maguchia kuchka*, the 'powerful clique' as Stassov used to call the Five. I was, in fact, protesting against the picturesque in Russian music and against those who failed to see that the picturesque is produced by very small tricks.*

Touché. Manuel de Falla might have said, and certainly thought, exactly that. For him it would have been no less applicable to his own Spain. *Mavra*, though substantially preposterous in its activities, is important in defining Stravinsky's relationship to his Russian inheritance after he had already become the great contemporary cosmopolitan of music. Its mild archaism, *démodé* music as Stravinsky himself

* Expositions and Developments (Faber & Faber, London)

dubbed it, also in its way has its echoes in Falla. The precise definition may not be the same, and there is nothing preposterous in any composition by Falla. All the same, both the echoes and the lack of the preposterous tell us one more small thing about Manuel de Falla.

As in *The Three Cornered Hat* and the *Fantasía baetica* Falla used regional dances and songs, so in *El retablo* and the harpsichord concerto he does the same. But not the same: in the *Hat* there is seguidillas, fandango, farruca and jota; and in the *Fantasía* there is sevillanas to start with and later there is copla. But in *El retablo* and the concerto the references are historical rather than regional. *El retablo* has gallardas, romances and other matter from the Middle Ages and from the Spanish 'Golden Century'. But just as he had transformed the regional dances in the earlier works and integrated them into his own autonomous style, so he did the same, even more comprehensively, with the classical and Romanesque elements in his later compositions. Thus a kind of overall homogeneity is preserved all through, the totality of the creative process undiluted.

In *El retablo* Falla turned finally from the colourful, exotic and obviously 'popular' elements of the Andalucían works to the larger, less particular, more universal idioms of Castile; and in so doing he became more than ever the musical embodiment of the Spanish soul, the total Spanish consciousness.

Yet once again one has to be careful in making these divisions and sub-divisions: they are fundamentally artificial and have only a limited relevance. Falla's declared intention was to unify the whole of Spanish music, with its varied regional and central variants, into a single universal style that could take its place in the European mainstream; to do, that is, what Bartók was doing for Hungary and Janáček for Moravia. In the process of accomplishing this he became more not less Spanish as he turned from the songs and dances and *evocación* of the sunny south to the hard, austere, aristocratic north. It was more than a relative shift of direction, a bias of geography. And it was in no sense a musical 'reaction', but a process of natural and, in the specific context, inevitable evolution.

Technically, much of the unique sound of *El retablo* derives from a further extension of the theory of natural resonance. But it also derives from Falla's extreme subtlety and originality of scoring, a refinement of the mastery of orchestration pinpointed in *The Three Cornered Hat*; reduced, frequently abstracted, the more limited resources used with great precision and a fastidious care for the smallest detail. Yet, again, this fastidiousness and extreme care does not, as it so easily could, result in devitalization. Indeed, the sheer vitality of Falla's late music, the harpsichord concerto no less than *El retablo*, is one of its most memorable characteristics, as the sense of red passion is in the earlier works. Once more one has to ask a question in the face of an apparent contradiction. Just as Falla's understanding of and sympathy for the women in his compositions seems at variance with his withdrawn and celibate life, so the dark passion and surge of his 'Andalucían' works and the razor sharp vitality of all of them but especially the later ones seems no less at odds with the delineations of his character. So how was it that this punctilious little man who hardly, if at all, seemed to have touched the rough and raw edges of life came to compose music of such sparkling vitality and uninhibited passion? With most men the closer you get to them the clearer they appear. But with others, and Manuel de Falla is an obvious example, proximity and efforts at penetration and analysis only deepen and complicate the enigma, open rather than close the distance between themselves and an increase of understanding. It is the same with the novelist E. M. Forster, another enigmatic character.

And it is no use saying that it is precisely within that apparent dichotomy that the tensions which go into the making of an artist and a vital art originated. That is to make a statement but not to commit oneself to a fruitful analysis leading to fuller understanding. It obscures rather than clarifies the central riddle. It is true so far as it goes; but it doesn't go anywhere worthwhile.

In certain respects Falla as the musical embodiment of Spain is a contradiction. But then Spain herself is something of a contradiction. The Spaniard, especially the southern

Spaniard, tends to be verbose, assertive, often arrogant, a dreamer of huge monolithic dreams. And all of these things Manuel de Falla was not. Typically, the true Spanish composer should be the prolix Albéniz. And in the narrow sense perhaps he is. And Albéniz too had begun to refine and economize his style in his last work, his masterpiece *Iberia*. But again, it is the southern Spaniard who is typified by Albéniz. Falla goes farther and deeper. He represents the total Spaniard, the perdurable one that lies below the surface of the other, attractive, engaging and incorrigible though that other is. Falla himself, like the eternal Spain he speaks of and for, is something of a paradox and a contradiction. It is part of what makes him so completely Spanish.

El retablo de Maese Pedro is, like *L'Histoire du Soldat*, a 'narrative work'; that is to say, the action is carried forward by a narrator, but unlike *Les Noces* which, again according to Stravinsky's own description, resembles James Joyce's *Ulysses* in that it aims to present rather than describe, *El retablo* and *L'Histoire* are overtly descriptive. Indeed, the Spanish term for the Boy, and the one used by Falla in the score, is *Trujamán*, which means more correctly 'interpreter'; his rôle is to elucidate to a simple uneducated but perceptive audience the action of the Puppet Show. So far involved is he that from time to time he has to be reprimanded by Master Peter, even by Don Quixote himself, for holding up or confusing the goings on by interjecting comments and asides of his own. This is not exactly the rôle of the Narrator in *L'Histoire du Soldat*; but the two conceptions obviously originated in the same area of the creative imagination.

In view of this and a number of other affinities of a loose and largely unconnected but still relevant kind, it is curious to find that Stravinsky, according to Pahissa, declared that although he greatly admired Falla, 'he follows a very different path from mine'. Remembering Stravinsky's words concerning *Mavra* quoted above, it would seem that the two of them followed very similar paths, even if Stravinsky's fecundity and Falla's sparsity of output appear in sharp contrast. But perhaps that in itself was part of the divergence. Stravinsky's widespread plundering of the entire world of music, ancient and modern, throughout a long active career, had nothing to do with Falla's lifelong single-mindedness. If Stravinsky's aim was wide and comprehensive, Falla's was narrow and concentrated. All the same, it is not so divergent as all that; the magpie mind of Igor Stravinsky had its cool hard centre that held firm through all the years of his compositional activity. It was only the outer part of him that perpetually seemed to alter where it alteration found. But no part of Manuel de Falla exhibited that propensity for alteration. It is a difference in kind as well as degree.

The essence of Falla's mature style is most completely exposed in the Concerto for Harpsichord and Chamber Orchestra. The full title is of some significance. It is: 'Concierto per Clavicembalo (o Pianoforte), Flauto, Oboe, Clarinetto, Violino e Violoncello'. But even here is some ambivalence. The concerto is dedicated to Wanda Landowska and was again conceived with that great artist's strong and fiery style particularly in mind. The substitution of piano for harpsichord, though on the surface permissible, is another of those solecisms which even the toughest and most uncompromising artists seem curiously heir to. It not only detracts from the concerto's true character: it absolutely contravenes it. A note on the published score requires that, as in *El retablo*, the tone of the harpsichord shall be as sonorous as possible. In no sense is this a piece of chamber music with clavier obbligato. Falla's intentional use of harpsichord rather than the piano with its thicker, woollier tone, both here and in *El retablo*, was quite deliberate, even though he performed the concerto in Paris in both forms and from published accounts scored a considerable success. Not only does the harpsichord impart a brighter, more glittering tone to the texture, abstract the music's particular emotional and intellectual essence in a way no other medium can, it also serves to emphasize the harmonic structure by its crispness and lack of tonal 'overhang'. Substitution of the piano takes the tang out of the harmony and the bite out of the rhythm and tends to blur the sharp-edged outlines.

The concerto is another spare and ascetic work, though again one of immense vitality. In this it is entirely in keeping with Falla's overall life and artistic credo at the time of its composition. The extended slow movement, placed between two vigorous outer ones, the first a brilliant toccata, the third a vivid dance, is the real heart of the matter. This great liturgical creation with its sonorous pealing of bells and deep organ points, bears the inscription (*A. Dom. MCM. In Festo Corporis Christi*) on its final page—a clear indication of its origins and provenance.

All Falla's intensity of religious feeling went into this magnificent movement, all his burning Spanish pride and fervour. It is the ultimate justification for the view that virtually every one of his compositions is fundamentally religious and liturgical in the broadest sense. Yet its original inspiration did not come from any religious experience or prompting: it came instead from the venue of a meeting of the Academia de la Historica in Madrid, where some pictures of outsize guitars on the walls of the room gave Falla the clue he needed. It was no more than that: it didn't have to be. It is a familiar process. As always, in the process of creation the artist needs hints and suggestions, igniting sparks rather than detailed expositions. Too much hampers the imagination. It is Henry James's *donnée*, the ears closed deliberately to anything but that. So the outsize guitars provided the spark, the 'germ', the *donnée*. Therein lay the genesis of those great sweeps of broken chords and huge arpeggios in this slow movement.

The whole concerto is informed with the full fruits of the technique of natural resonance. Falla had used this technique frequently all along, and in *El retablo* he had erected it into a comprehensive system. Here, in the Concerto for Harpsichord, he brought the process to its consummation. The juxtaposition of major and minor chords is now only apparent. The music is not entrenched in tonality at all. If we rid our minds of the habit of thinking (and hearing) in terms of major and minor key centres, and think instead of the series of natural harmonics, not only in specific places or passages, but all through, the entire concerto appears in quite a different light. It was no doubt for this reason that the note prefacing the score also contains Falla's express instruction that all the instruments must be soloists and that on no account must the strings be doubled. If the instrumental forces are in any way inflated, the precise function of each note in the chord may become obscured and the underlying harmonic, melodic and rhythmic structure confused and distorted. The same argument applies against the substitution of piano for harpsichord.

The harpsichord concerto represents Falla's final achievement in his search for a universal style based upon Spanish national resources. It is also the most uncompromisingly Spanish of all his compositions, certainly all but *El retablo* which is in many respects linked to it technically and stylistically as well as ethnically and so must be seen as running in parallel and as natural complement, the two representing twin aspects of the Spanish 'thing in itself'. It is not simply that even here there is, at (3) in the first movement, a direct quotation from a fifteenth-century popular song from Castile, 'De los alamos vengo, Madre' which in fact forms the thematic germ or motif of the entire work. The presence of an actual popular melody in any Falla work is so rare as to constitute a notable exception. It is far more that the whole concerto is permeated by an intensely Spanish spirit, the universal historic spirit of Spain, the epitome of all that is or can be meant by the generic terms 'Spain' and 'Spanish', which reaches its climax and fulfilment in the profoundly religious Lento. The two quick outer movements, Allegro, 2/4, and Vivace (flessible, scherzando), 6/8, are usually taken as demonstrating Falla's indebtedness to Domenico Scarlatti whose lucidity of musical thought and elegance of style he greatly admired. And so maybe they are; yet the overall idiom is unmistakably modern, its stylistic salute to the past in full sympathy with Stravinsky's ideals of the period (1926). The connection with Scarlatti is probably fortuitous: any Spanish keyboard composition with a dash of wit and sparkle is inclined to be dubbed 'Scarlattian'. There is no doubt that Falla admired Scarlatti; but it probably did not go much farther than that.

Again, *L'Histoire du Soldat* comes to mind, not in the aesthetic conception or the dramatic concept, which are totally different, obviously, but in the instrumental sonorities. Yet even here it is necessary to be wary of the careless use of language, for Stravinsky's harmonic idiom was in no way similar to Falla's, and it is the harmonic idiom above all, the extended use of the technique of natural resonance, that gives the Falla concerto its unique sonority. And it is the sonority that makes the Concerto for Harpsichord endlessly intriguing.

Yet the so-called 'neo-classicism' is not, *vide* Constant Lambert, in the least chilly or remote: it is not in fact properly described as 'neo-classical' at all, any more than the harmonic idiom of the concerto is correctly described as bi-tonal or polytonal. The roots are sunk deep into a fertile soil, the resulting effect altogether different from Stravinsky's manifold evolutions.

But above all, and it cannot be too often insisted upon, the *Concierto para clavicembalo* must be seen as the final justification of those ideals which fired its composer in the far-off days when, as a young student full of passionate fervour he came under the fructifying influence of Felipe Pedrell. If we place this concerto and *El retablo* beside the best works of Falla's contemporaries and immediate successors—Albéniz, Granados, Turina—we can hardly avoid being struck by the truth that whereas the others were, maybe in their own different ways but still unarguably, little more than purveyors of the picturesque and the regional, if not the unashamedly parochial, Falla broke through the circumscribing bonds of narrow and exclusive nationalism and gave the music of Spain a universal voice it had largely lost since the Golden Age of the sixteenth century.

Ann Livermore draws attention to the relevance of the poems of Ruben Dario, the Nicaraguan poet whose influential *Cantos de Vida Esperanza* were published in Madrid in 1905, to Falla's artistic development. This may well be so, and perhaps even more than is generally supposed. Falla was always deeply sensitive to literary and other influences. Partly because of this and partly because of certain intimations in Pahissa's biography, the idea has circulated that Falla was first tempted towards a career in literature. But there is nothing exceptional in this. If it was so, he was by no means unique. A number of musicians and writers of a markedly visual cast of imagination have hovered between music, literature and painting. Arnold Bax is a case in point, a man of literary as well as musical gifts; but it in no way alters the fact that the basic and significant faculty is for music, and can only fulfil itself ultimately in musical terms. No one, to turn it another way, who has read the life of William Hazlitt will fail to recognize the way in which a creative faculty is often composite, its operation not immediately decided but its ultimate direction and fulfilment, in retrospect, never in real doubt.

Ms Livermore outlines the internal and external connections and relationships; and it seems likely, to say no more, that Dario's poetry influenced both the *Nights in the Gardens of Spain* (Ronald Crichton notes this connection too, as well as the French poet Francis Jammes) and the Concerto for Harpsichord. It is even suggested that the original idea for the concerto's slow movement derived from reading Dario.

If the poems of Ruben Dario did in fact have a bearing on both these compositions, some interesting speculations arise, since nothing could be farther in style and overall aesthetic from the *Nights* than the concerto. On the other hand, if that dual correspondence is true and valid, then it would appear further to emphasize the fundamental unity of Falla's creative faculty throughout his active career.

The sonority of the Concerto for Harpsichord is unique, and the cause of it lies, as I have said, in the technique of natural resonance which Falla consummated in this work. But it is also due to the way in which Falla brings together the old Spanish music with its characteristic tone and ambience and the particular assumptions in respect of texture and sonority expected and required by the contemporary ear.

Indeed, Falla's late music suggests in some respects that he might be going the way of Webern rather than of Stravinsky. In one sense, and probably the most important, he was not going the way of anyone but himself. He was, partly because of his own temperament, partly because of the position of Spain and her music in relation to the European whole when he first started to compose, an isolated and a lonely figure, certainly a man determined (in both senses) to tread his own path, follow his own star. And in that too he was entirely Spanish.

But no man, certainly no artist, can or wishes to live and work in a vacuum. Nothing in Falla's history suggests that, as a musician, he was uninvolved in, let alone uninterested in or unaware of, everything that was going on in the musical world around him. Indeed, the opposite is more nearly the truth. Therefore the relating of Falla's works outside themselves and their immediate context is not only valid but necessary; his ideal of founding a universal Spanish musical style demands and requires it.

I have said that in his late music Falla appears to be going the way of Webern rather than Stravinsky, or Schoenberg, or even Bartók. By this I do not mean that it is like Webern, either technically or stylistically; but from the point of view of the finer musical aesthetic there is a twin direction emerging. In the search for brevity, concision and absolute purity of style Falla and Webern were moving on adjacent courses. Stravinsky's description of Webern as a cutter of exquisite diamonds might, with a slightly altered bias, be applied also to Falla in his late compositions.

This is particularly evident in two tiny works which lie either side of the concerto, two little pieces of totally differing character, one of extreme delicacy, the other declamatory and dramatic, but each demonstrating at least one significant detail of Falla's mature manner and technique.

The first, *Psyché*, is a setting of words by the French poet and musical writer Georges Jean-Aubry, which many have seen as a deliberate assumption of the French style. But this is hardly a sustainable argument, at least on the purely musical side. To be sure, the texture of the vocal line is nothing like that in *El retablo*, or even *La vida breve* at its most Falla-ish. It is not even like that of the succeeding small work, the *Soneto a Córdoba*; perhaps least of all like that. On the other hand, it is hardly worth noting that it is not like any of these. A sensitive artist is not likely to use a decisively Spanish declaration when his original text is French. But listen to the instrumental textures—they are straight in line with those in the concerto, and the relevant part of *El retablo*. The weaving flute line does not precisely outline the same contours as the violin (or flute and oboe) in *El retablo* (or *El amor brujo*) ; and the largely staccato and 'vertical' style of the concerto does not leave room for melodic arabesques or flowing delineations. Yet the inner correspondence is not to be missed if the ear, aided by the eye on the score, attends to what is written instead of what has been said to have been written.

Psyché, small though it is, is important to Falla's total opus and may suggest that had he continued to compose with some regularity after the concerto this Webern-like miniaturism might well have been one direction in which he would have proceeded. On his own terms and not Webern's or anyone else's of course.

The *Soneto a Córdoba* might also be referred to Webern who, despite certain unsupported assumptions of unfailing 'exquisiteness' could also be dramatic and declamatory, as in certain songs and the two cantatas. There is nothing of expressionism in Falla; but that is not the central point. Nor is Webern's mystical leaning analagous to Falla's; but that is not central either. What is central is a kind of aesthetic kernel by which similar artistic ends move on different though convergent routes, the arrival perhaps never actually achieved but the relativities discerned none the less.

As with Stravinsky, any connection between Falla and Webern cannot be pressed too far; probably not as far as with Stravinsky. Yet it need not be ignored, for there are movable currents at any time in which all artists are involved, and there are others in which some are involved; indeed in some cases even those who appear not to have much in common come together at certain points and those points may well be an important and significant terrain for both sides. Falla and Stravinsky is a commonplace of criticism; Falla and Webern is more tenuous and perhaps arguable; but it exists, and not only on the ground of physical dimension of particular works. Webern was an extremist; and Falla too was in his own and no less determined and uncompromising way an extremist. It goes farther than that; but it may also begin there.*

*See note 5

The *Soneto a Córdoba* was written in 1927 (*Psyché* was 1924; the concerto 1926). The occasion here was the tercentenary of the poet Luis de Góngora, the great master of the poetic Baroque. It apparently caused some passing astonishment that Falla, the austere and ascetic should set verses of such high-powered elaboration as Góngora's. But again this is to misunderstand. Although Falla was a Franciscan spirit and his natural historical period would seem to be that of the pre-Renaissance, the Middle Ages and the Romanesque, there was in him, in large part because he was a true-born Spaniard, that conflict and inner tension which did much to determine his personal and artistic nature as it has done much to form and fashion the Spanish soul itself. But it also represents an aspect of Baroque, where images of suffering and spiritual tension are one of its leading characteristics. Lying behind the elaborations, the frequent extravagances, conceits even, of Baroque is that central fact of internal tension and spiritual conflict. Therefore, apart from the obvious appeal of the occasion, as well as the enthusiastic advocacy of Federico Garcia Lorca and Gerardo Diego, there was no incompatibility or contradiction in Falla's setting of Góngora's homage to the city of his birth.

And indeed, the vocal line supported by harp of the *Soneto* demonstrates how true this was for him and how in setting Góngora's elaborate verses he not only did no outrage to his artistic beliefs and sensibilities, but in fact revealed more about himself.

The vocal line is, as I say, declamatory and dramatic, an admirable match for the poem. And the part for harp is complementary in a way that makes it absolutely essential. Again, Falla sanctioned the substitution of the piano, and again he played (and recorded) it thus himself. But as with the concerto the harpsichord is essential if it is to make its proper impression, so the *Soneto* must have its harp and not a piano.

Coupled with the concision and economy of the Concerto for Harpsichord, these two small vocal works might appear to indicate a direction for the future. But it did not work out like that. After the concerto, and the *Soneto* which is essentially an occasional piece, Falla ceased to publish. He did not cease to compose; but with one exception no new works appeared from him during the remaining years of his life. Even the exception is only partial. It refers to the suite of four pieces for orchestra collectively entitled *Homenajes*. But of these only one was in any sense new.

The first three were orchestrations of pieces written in homage to various musical friends and colleagues, two upon the occasions of their deaths, the other for a 70th birthday. The 'homenaje' he wrote for the memory of Debussy, for guitar, he now orchestrated to form part of the suite. In 1935 Paul Dukas, another who had befriended him in Paris before the First World War, had died, and Falla composed a brief late piano piece, *Pour le Tombeau de Paul Dukas*, in which his maturest style is deployed on a small but intense scale. (The preoccupation with death and the celebration of death was also part of the essentially Spanish cast of his temperament.) This short piece was also orchestrated to take its place in the final suite. The third item was a fanfare on the initials of the violinist and conductor, E. Fernandez Arbós, whose 70th birthday Falla wished to honour in recognition of Arbós's signal services to his own music. In view of Arbós's devoted work on behalf of other Spanish national composers, this tribute, part of a collection of fourteen by leading musicians of the day, was a token of gratitude on behalf of Spanish music as a whole. The fanfare appropriately opens the suite.

To end the suite Falla paid a last tribute to the man whose ideals had inspired not only himself but the whole movement towards a true Spanish national musical renaissance, Felipe Pedrell. Falla decided to weave a musical tapestry based on themes from Pedrell's unperformed opera *La Celestina*, composed in 1903. The result is curious. When he set to work on *Psyché* Falla had, according to his frequent custom, created in his imagination a scene of a courtly concert in the Tocador de la Reina in the Alhambra in 1730, during the reign of Philip V and Queen Elisabeta. Now he again showed how closely he liked to work from a literary and pictorial basis by imagining in his mind a setting of courtly lords and ladies

in the style of the frescoes by Orcagna at Pisa. With this
background and out of the themes of Pedrell's opera, Falla
wove his musical tapestry—and that is the right term: it is
a tapestry.

Unhappily, something appeared to go wrong. Frankly,
'Pedrelliana' is pretty enough; but it is a feeble piece, lacking
both the passion and imaginative vitality of all Falla's best
music. It is said that he deliberately subordinated his own
personality to that of Pedrell; but if that is so, it does small
homage to the man usually taken to be the great inspirer
of modern Spanish music. So the question has inevitably
to be asked: Were Falla's own powers in decline, or was
Pedrell after all a composer of no real distinction? That
Pedrell was a scholar and musicologist of intense dedication
and integrity is not to be doubted; but as a composer it
would seem to be a different matter, otherwise how could
he have been the progenitor of such undernourished music?
For this in any context is the smallest of small beer; the
weakest and most diluted of Spanish musical wine. It intro-
duces some pleasant court music of the Middle Ages and
at a far remove recreates the world of the Romanesque. But
unlike *El retablo* which refers to broadly the same historical
periods, it neither revives what Thomas Mann, apropos of
Don Quixote, called 'the noble madness of chivalry', nor
vitalizes in contemporary terms the old Spanish courtly
world. Technically it shows some subtlety of harmony and
orchestration; otherwise it is totally indecisive, if mildly agreeable. But that is something which can never be said of any
other music composed and published by Manuel de Falla.
It is very far from being his *Parsifal*.

Nor in all probability was it ever intended so to be. That
distinction, if it is a valid conjecture at all, belongs, or should
have belonged to the huge choral/orchestral project, *Atlántida*,
upon which he intermittently worked over the remaining
twenty years of his life.

Ill health and preoccupation continually troubled him:
Atlántida was always about to be finished, but never was.
It remained a torso, albeit a substantial one, at the time of
his death. And, fastidious to the last, he would allow nothing

of the music he had composed to appear while he still lived. He is reported to have considered once a 'trial run' of parts of it, but immediately shied away from that possibility, fearing that adverse criticism might inhibit his capacity to complete the whole. And in that decision he was probably right: musical history does not encourage the idea that piece-meal presentation of works intended to be unified wholes does them any sort of good in the long run. It is one of the ironies of his own history that because he did not live to complete it himself, *Atlántida* had after all to be given incomplete and in the end 'finished' by another hand.

Unlike the apparently mythical eighth symphony of Sibelius, a great deal of the music of *Atlántida* not only existed but was known to exist. After his death, the material passed into the hands of Falla's family, his brother and sister, upon whose decision the work of correlation and completion was entrusted to Falla's most dedicated pupil, Ernesto Halffter. But for many years, until around 1960, it was shrouded in mystery. When at last it was given its 'première', in a concert version in Barcelona in 1961, it had to be in a 'made up' edition and proved to be a sad disappointment to those who had been led to expect the final testament to the genius of its composer in his lifelong search for a truly Spanish international style.

Perhaps we expected too much. More likely, *Atlántida* when it did at last appear in public was not altogether what Falla had intended, and what he himself would have published had he lived to complete the total grand design himself. He seems actually to have completed rather less than was at first supposed, although he left many sketches and projected ideas; a large mass of material which even the most devoted of his followers could only bring together by a certain amount of speculative guesswork. Even a stage performance at La Scala, Milan, in June 1962, under Thomas Schippers, though nearer to Falla's intention, did not significantly alter the situation. Nor did the final, shortened and 'definitive' edition, again made by Ernesto Halffter and given in Lucerne in 1976, resolve the enigma.*

*See Appendix I

Here again Falla's lifelong habits of secrecy rebound against him. Thus what was first presented, and what was later given after further thought, revision and re-editing, was clearly not in fact what Falla had been striving for. Perhaps at the time of his death he still did not have the whole project clear in his own mind. It seems certain that *Atlántida* as he worked upon it grew and expanded far beyond its original conception. Many sections were added as he went along: conception and execution both became considerably enlarged through the twenty years of its labours. And if it had not become perfectly clear in his own mind, it was unlikely to become so in anyone else's. What has been revealed and performed is not Falla's unadulterated conception; so we have to accept the Concerto for Harpsichord as his last major word on the subject that lay closest to his heart.

If *Atlántida* was, as most of his friends and commentators believed, to have been the final summing up and ultimate justification of his life's work and pursuit of a specific ideal, it seems likely that we were robbed of a considerable master-piece by his inability to finish it. We know a good deal about his intentions; but that is not the same thing. It was conceived as a 'choreographic poem' for soloists, choir and orchestra, to words by the Catalan poet Jacinto Verdaguer. Alternatively it is described as a 'scenic cantata'. It is not all that important which is used or preferred: what is important, and is implied in both descriptions, is that *Atlántida* is essentially a work for the stage rather than the concert hall, and that only stage production can do it justice. One reason why Falla refused to allow performance of parts during his lifetime was that it would have had to be 'without décor'. *Atlántida* was always in its creator's mind a scenic work, not a straight cantata or oratorio, the 'décor' not only important but an essential part of it and its true inner meaning.*

The visual, 'décor' side of *Atlántida* derives from Falla's friendship with the painter José María Sert whose Baroque-style frescoes gave him many ideas through the years and a voluminous correspondence.† When Sert died in 1938, Falla

*See note 6
†See Appendix I

said he felt free to concentrate on the music. But there is no possible doubt that he never changed his mind that *Atlántida* was indeed a 'scenic cantata', with the 'scenic' as important as the 'cantata'.

The 'purity' and austerity of Falla's late style is evident from much of the music which did finally appear. By no means everything of quality is lost, and some of the music, enough and more to increase our regret that the great project never did come to complete fruition, is of a high standard of excellence. But somewhere stylistic unity evolved from a comprehensive musical synthesis of all the various regional idioms of Spain appears to have proved elusive, or at least misjudged. *Atlántida* did not after all turn out to be the triumphant vindication of all that its composer had lived and worked for. We may regret the circumstances that prevented Falla from completing it himself; but there is nothing more we can do about it. All that could be done has been done. What became evident is that only Falla could compose Falla's music. We could have inferred it from everything that he did complete.

Despite the ambivalence of *Atlántida* as we eventually received it, the music that Falla composed up to 1927 is enough to confirm him as the outstanding modern Spanish composer. We may assert with confidence that he succeeded as no others did with anything like the same mastery in transcending narrow and exclusive nationalism and achieved the universality of style and the international idiom which brought Spanish music back into the European mainstream after more than three centuries in the backwaters. He was not enslaved by his national inheritance but liberated by it, as it was liberated by him; or should have been had his successors, even one successor, been of anything approaching his own calibre. His total achievement has not always been properly understood because his musical contemporaries, as well as those who immediately preceded him and those who came later, in Spain seldom escaped from the dilemma of constricting nationalism. He has too often been mistakenly identified with a movement whose ideals he did not fundamentally share, or outgrew in the early stages of his career. He stands apart from the Albéniz-Granados-Turina school, even though they all strove towards a goal lesser than his but not dissimilar. No composer was more absolutely and essentially Spanish; yet he in no way exemplifies the nationalist who won't travel, as could be said for many years of even so potent a composer as Edward Elgar. He found a means of injecting his own musical personality into the broader current, and with it the essential spirit of his nation, the soul and mind of Spain at its most meaningful and most creative. He sought universality and international acceptance of his own and his country's music; and in the end he found and achieved both. It was the ultimate quality of his genius that set him apart from all the rest.

Falla was fundamentally an objective artist, as we have seen. That is to say, it is not in the end the whole man, the total personality, who presents himself to us so much as the impeccable artist. Of course, such a form of words is and always will be relative: the impeccable artist may well be the whole man, and if that is so then Manuel de Falla was a prime example. We have the strongest sense of an active personality in Falla. But one feels too that little if anything not germane to his evolution as an artist found its way into his compositions; nothing purely subjective or romantically personal. Elgar once said: 'I put the whole of myself into my music. I hold nothing back.' Falla, by contrast, held a good deal back, deliberately, even if it was only that which was not absolutely first rate. He was in many ways a recluse, a profoundly private man, musically as well as personally, existentially as well as biographically. Nothing extraneous mattered. Unlike Beethoven, or Wagner, or Elgar and Richard Strauss among his near contemporaries, Falla ruthlessly excised from his life and its activity everything that did not directly pertain to his art and its development. And always it gave him strength as well as limitation. He was a passionate idealist, and an uncompromising extremist in that; and his ideal was quite simply one of continual purification of thought and style. He achieved it, but only at some definable cost. The style was the man after all.

I have already outlined the way in which the histories

of Spanish and English music appear to run on roughly parallel lines. But at one point they differ sharply; and it was significant in the mutual period of the musical renaissances. The popular music of Spain has caught the general public imagination in a way that English folk music never has, or could. The reason is the more immediately exotic character of the former. A surfeit of Spanish musical *vin ordinaire*, with its insistent tang and sandy flavour, may be in the long run as monotonous and as enervating as a surfeit of English pentatonic musical thick soup; but to begin with the Spanish variety is more stimulating, certainly more lively and colourful. Maybe this, in both cases, is more or less on the surface; but it is what lies upon the surface that frequently determines the direction a national artform may take, and initially have to take. *La vida breve* or *Hugh The Drover*, the one essentially Spanish, the other essentially English. But there is no doubt where the casual ear is first taken.

Falla outstripped the inhibiting influence of folk music for its own sake. He did not turn his back on it; he simply went to the roots and found there larger and more universal truths about his heritage than those that lay nearest the surface. He freed Spanish music from the persistent stamping of feet and clacking of castanets by assimilating them into a style that finally emerged as more than ever comprehensively Spanish. His music does not depend upon local colour only, not even his earlier music; and as he advanced along his chosen path it was still not totally expurgated but became ever more subtle and concealed. He is one of the few consciously 'national' composers who escaped from the nationalist cul-de-sac. Elgar never took the same starting point and so was not confronted with the same problem, at least not in anything like the same form. Vaughan Williams did, and he achieved his own solution. Falla is closer in this respect to Vaughan Williams (and to Bartók) than to Elgar who more nearly resembles Sibelius in expressing a national spirit without resource to endemically national popular idioms. But Vaughan Williams was in no way a 'purist'. Hence the largely untidy music of Vaughan Williams and the smaller, discriminating music of Falla.

But in the end none of that is a criterion of artistic value. Restricted though it is, the value of Falla's music lies in its unswerving idealism and in the passionate intensity with which that ideal was pursued and ultimately realized. Falla could not have been a prolific composer, for his entire artistic being depended on a rigorous selectivity. We have to accept him as he was, or we cannot appreciate him at all. To ask for a more garrulous Falla is to ask for another man and composer altogether. And that is neither intelligent nor to the point. He lived and worked as he had to live and work. Any other view is critically inane. We must never, here or elsewhere, be sidetracked from the kernel of the nut.

On the score of *Psyché* he meticulously described himself as 'Musicien d'Espagne, natif de la Cité de Cadix, en Andaloufie'. In that he spoke total truth, even if he spoke it in French rather than his native Spanish; as true as Debussy when he referred to himself as 'musicien français'. But Debussy's *mot* was uttered during the First World War, when France was under threat and a gesture of defiance was not only in order but expected as part of the order of the day, any day. Falla's was more generally relevant. And it is significant perhaps that it appears on that minor masterpiece in which he is often taken to have donned the mantle of the French style; if only for that specific occasion. I have already put that idea in its place; but the fact of the declaration remains and must be noted.

Falla has always been accepted as the most exceptional musical spokesman of Spain in this country. But his impact on the international music scene has been less than it might and should have been. His technique of natural resonance could in other circumstances have exerted a potent alternative influence on the evolution of modern music as a whole; alternative to Schoenberg's seriality and its overall consequences, and also to Stravinsky's magpie cosmopolitanism. Indeed, if he had composed more, especially after the twin poles of *El retablo* and the Concerto for Harpsichord had finally established him as free of the restrictive nationalist taint, he could well have exerted an influence as widespread as that of Stravinsky himself, certainly as significant as that of Bartók.

But he was not born to influence, to lead and dominate in that sense. He was a private, intensely motivated but inner directed and fanatically meticulous man of Spain, all Spain; Spain in the totality of her historical and her modern assumptions. It is in that rather than his capacity for influencing people and projecting creative sponsorships that his ultimate value must lie. And perhaps that in itself tells something more about him personally, but still more about Spain.

V

HOW BLIND AN ALLEY?

THE CONSENSUS OF opinion is that the nationalist composer (or indeed any type of 'national' artist) must eventually find himself in a creative cul-de-sac. This has in practice often proved to be the case; but it is not necessarily so. The composer who is big enough resolves the problem more or less automatically before he is ever trapped in it. He (or she) in fact achieves from a national basis precisely that universality of idiom and appeal to which in the case of Spain and Spanish music Manuel de Falla devoted his life and his talent. The other major figure who comes to mind in the European context is Béla Bartók. It has seldom been suggested that Bartók's genius was inhibited and in the end stifled by his strong nationalistic leanings throughout his life. If Stravinsky, on account of his needle sharp-wittedness, seems the most likely musical associate, and if on a more esoteric plane Webern pointed a general way Falla himself had begun to indicate he might perhaps go on his own terms, from the nationalist point of view it is Bartók who runs in closest parallel. Falla's and Bartók's attitude to and creative use of national folk material was notably similar. And Magyar folk music, though different in character from the Spanish variety (though both at certain levels have strong gypsy associations), has an immediately identifiable and 'catchy' rhythmic bite and melodic exoticism. I have mentioned Vaughan Williams also; but because of the particular cast of the English temperament—W. B. Yeats's perceptive remark, 'The English mind is meditative, rich, deliberate; it may remember the Thames Valley', gives the clue—English folk song is softer, less hard edged than either Spanish or Magyar so that its use inevitably produces a different effect. The relationship to Vaughan Williams is therefore of a somewhat different order. But he too was one who forged a personal outgoing musical idiom out of the basic elements of folk song. His connection with Falla is historical as much as contemporary; it lies in the fusion of folk elements with those of the Golden Age of the sixteenth century, which only to a very limited extent can be said of Bartók.

It is thus entirely wrong to assert that Falla 'dried up' and ceased to compose (or at least to publish) because the impasse of artistic nationalism in the end defeated him, or to say that any who came after him at whatever remove had to start where he himself 'had left off'. Falla had already broken that impasse, both for himself and for his successors. The Concerto for Harpsichord in particular, has left any danger of a narrow and inhibiting nationalism behind, just as Bartók's best music is deeply infused with his own passionate Hungarian spirit but can in no sense be held to approach a nationalistic impasse or cul-de-sac.

The reasons for Falla's long years of virtual creative silence are both various and in many ways mysterious. But one thing they are not is the result of nationalistic inhibition. A work like *El retablo* may seem to the careless glance to be more nationalistic than universal/international; but in fact that is not the case. The basic musical language is in no way narrowly nationalist; it is national in the true and liberating sense, the sense that is the total opposite of the 'folk' and the picturesque/domestic.

It is the use of the Spanish language in a particularly generic manner that stamps *El retablo* with unequivocal nationality, the wholly original but absolutely endemic declamation. But there is nothing new or remarkable in that: if you compose to a particular language and do not find the correct declamation to support and complement it, you are simply making a bad setting. This is a principle as old as music itself; it has only incidentally to do with the romantic nationalism of the nineteenth century. It only became a problem and an issue where the musical tradition had grown weak and a kind of nebulous and vaguely accepted musical *lingua franca* of no particular distinction had replaced or been substituted for a natural and spontaneous declamation required by the native speech. It was never a problem in Germany or Italy, yet the smallest attention to German and Italian music will show how naturally and almost unconsciously the melodic delineation accepts and supports the curve and inflexion of the language. It is for this reason that opera and oratorio in any but the original language must contravene the totality of the work, however devotedly and with whatever skill and care the translation is made and presented. This is a contentious subject; but it is also one that is still not given its full and proper weight of argument.

Because of its nature and the venue for which it was written, a private theatre, and the consequent physical determination thus laid upon it, *El retablo* is in a sense an inevitably 'one off' work. Theoretically, there is no reason why Falla, or anyone else as gifted, should not have produced a number of *El retablo*s, just as Stravinsky could have written further *Mavra*s or *Histoire du Soldat*s. But that remains a matter of speculation. Such works serve a specific purpose at a specific time; neither their creators nor the international audience for which they were projected require or even admit drawn-out repetitions.

Yet in the larger sense, *El retablo* might easily have come to hold a very different position in the evolution of modern Spanish music. It has in it every ingredient for the founding of a potent school of Spanish opera. I refer of course to the idiom and the style, not to the subject matter. What Janáček did for Czech opera a more prolific Falla, or one who did not stand more or less alone in the quality of his genius, could have done for Spanish opera. Yet that is probably to go the wrong way about it. Falla gave the lead; he did not need to be more prolific himself. But there were no successors to take up that advantage, and Falla, as we are agreed, could not have been a more prolific composer without some drastic alteration of his essential nature and a radical modification of his creative chemistry.

But again, that is not the real point; and it is not in the end all that important. What matters is that Falla, with *El retablo* in particular, achieved a Spanish style and declamation

for the operatic medium which had no real following because there was no one to follow. Yet it was anything
but a dead end. The process had in fact begun in practice
with *La vida breve* but had its origins even farther back with
Pedrell. *El retablo* was the culmination of a long process.
If there was, as at some point in any national progress there
is bound to be, the threat of an impasse leading to a blind
alley, Falla in the Spanish context had broken through the
barrier and left the way open for further development.

His own years of creative silence then are not to be explained
away on any kind of nationalist ticket. *Atlántida* and declining
health kept him occupied for the better part of twenty years.
But there is nothing to suggest, let alone insist, that the
nationalist impasse was the cause of the decline in productivity
or the reason for the non-completion of what was intended
to be his masterwork. Indeed, the opposite is more nearly
the revealed truth: he was so intent on making *Atlántida*
the final justification of his own life and of his service to his
country's music that the task slowly grew out of his hand
and defeated in the end his best will, his ultimate intention.
But a cul-de-sac? No: that way lies illusion and the blindest
of blind alleys.

When it comes to instrumental rather than vocal or operatic
music, however loosely defined, it is once more the Concerto
for Harpsichord that moves to the fore. The concision of
this work was characteristic not only of Falla himself, not
only of Spanish music which, as we have seen can be unnervingly loquacious, but rather of the Latin temperament. Or
let us say that the forms most favoured in the Latin countries,
outside theatre music and to some extent even there, do not
uninhibitedly run in the direction of either large-scale abstract
compositions or of grandiose autodramatic turbulences. That
is, the symphonic tradition, whether running to Sibelian
severity of logic or Mahlerian total inclusion, belongs principally to the Austro-German or the Scandinavian cultures.
It has a very limited place, if any at all, in the Latin environ-
ments, for although there are French and Italian symphonies
they tend to differ significantly from the Austro-German or
Scandinavian varieties.

The case of Sibelius is interesting here. At first a symphonist of expansiveness and the large gesture, Sibelius subsequently brought symphonic form into line with contemporary musical and aesthetic thinking in general. He pared down the extravagances until there was hardly a trace of them left, the opulences, the old grand manner of a departed world, and produced, most notably in the Fourth Symphony, a conciseness and taut structural logic which, while couched in apparently traditional terms, moved decisively into the world of the twentieth century. The 'density' of which Schoenberg liked to speak in relation to modern music, his own in particular, was by no means his singular possession or invention. Nor did he ever claim that it was: it was a basic condition of contemporary thought and feeling and it took varying forms in different contexts. One was in Sibelius; another was Manuel de Falla. In extremis it claimed Anton Webern as its most uncompromising disciple.

Sibelius astutely solved, or evaded, the nationalist problem by composing a series of 'nationalistic' tone poems alongside his symphonies. He made a deliberate distinction between the two, between that is the symphonies as compositions worked out in terms of pure musical logic and the tone poems 'inspired by our national folk poetry'. To some extent he deceived himself, for no man can split or compartmentalize his work in that way, and inevitably the symphonies contain national elements while the tone poems have their strict formal logic. But the distinction made by Sibelius has a general relevance even if the specific one tends to be somewhat questionable. Nor, for Sibelius, was there any kind of impasse or blind alley. His two last major works represent the high points of each of the categories he defined. The Seventh Symphony and *Tapiola* lie side by side, each in its own field epitomising the composer's overall achievement.

But for Sibelius the problem was in any case less demanding. Finnish folk music, song and dance, has none of the quickly identifiable character of that of Spain, or Hungary. No doubt it has its recognizable inflexions, and a number of melodic and rhythmic characteristics can be isolated from it. Yet there is nothing there to stamp the place and culture of origin as there is with the popular music of Spain. The perils of musical nationalism are not spot-lighted by Sibelius, though he solved it as convincingly as he needed to, but by Bartók and Falla. For both the latter it was always a totally different problem, precisely because of the nature of the folk music of Hungary and Spain, the sharp delineations which are unmistakable and easy to parody. Thus for Bartók, as for Falla, the problem was distinct from that of Sibelius; and indeed, the only real connection between Bartók and Sibelius is that each found a valid way of evolving sonata form in the twentieth century in a direction that was convincing and avoided the formal doodling of most composers who tried to use sonata form as though it had not been moribund for a hundred years. Sibelius in his symphonies, Bartók in his string quartets, made the only true progress in this direction creatively admissible since the death of Beethoven.

In the matter of musical nationalism therefore, Falla moves in alongside Bartók while Sibelius remains entrenched in his northern fastness, with Carl Nielsen in a slightly different and in a sense tangential position nearby. But the problem for Falla was in any case never primarily formal. He did not allow himself to become sidetracked with the externals of sonata form, nor did he try, as both Sibelius and Bartók successfully did, to enlarge the scope of that form so that it once more became, in a greatly modified if not actually mutated sense, creatively viable. But for all that, he was never at a loss for a convincing structure for his compositions. His formal logic was complete and decisive, an unfailing match for the content of his works. But it bore no relationship, nor did it ever aspire to, to sonata form or to 'symphonic thinking' in general.

Sibelius, like Falla, ended his life with a prolonged period of virtual silence, out of which was long rumoured to come forth a new symphony. But it never materialized, despite frequently renewed expectations. Yet Sibelius was turned 60 when he ceased to produce new compositions, and behind him was a body of work sufficient to justify any active lifetime. The impression we have of extended silence from Sibelius was principally because of the great length of his life: he was over 90 when he died. There are historical precedents for a composer producing masterpieces in extreme old age, or giving up quite early and devoting the rest of his life to enjoying himself. Verdi is the prime example of the former, Rossini of the latter. But Falla belongs to neither category, nor is he linked to any other case or type. He constitutes a case on his own.

There is, however, another reason why Falla stands alone. He stands alone because Spain herself stood alone during his lifetime. Sibelius was inspired to national as well as international creation by Finnish history, in particular by the long Russian oppression of Finland and the struggle of the Finns to achieve liberation and independent nationhood: and Hungary was constantly threatened both politically and militarily, first under the Austro-Hungarian empire and later by Germany. In each case the fight for independence was of a kind that invariably leads to a great upsurge of national feeling and national aspiration with its reflection, sometimes its creation, in the arts. Thus Bartók, like Sibelius, had a point of focus for nationalist expression. But for Falla, as for any Spaniard, it was different. Spain was never threatened from the outside, was emotionally as well as geographically apart and independent. But internally Spain was in the worst possible situation, politically unstable and culturally in a backwater, the two closely interlinked if not actively cross-productive.

There is ample evidence that Falla was deeply disturbed by this national stagnation and widespread moral as well as intellectual corruption. A profoundly religious man, he was agonized by the persecution of the Church under the Republic; the prevailing anti-clericalicism and the burning of churches, the overall profanation of the whole of Spanish life. As the situation deteriorated and social disintegration set in generally during the 1930s, Falla was constantly on the point of moving from Granada to the more secure haven of Mallorca. He paid several visits to Palma without making any definite plans. But while there on one occasion he adapted the words of Verdaguer's *Balada de Mallorca* to the theme of the *andantino* section of Chopin's second Ballade, in F,

Op.38, for four part *a cappella* choir. The association of the
poet Verdaguer, whose *L'Atlántida* had already fertilized his
imagination, and the composer Chopin who spent some
famous months on the island with George Sand, gave Falla
an opportunity to take a little appropriate musical exercise.

But it was the situation on the Spanish mainland which
continued to trouble him. One result was his work during
the late 1920s and early 1930s in helping to organize festivals
of *cante jondo* and other traditional Spanish arts which he,
along with many of his compatriots, including the poet and
dramatist Federico Garcia Lorca, so tragically killed at the
outset of the Civil War, felt to be in increasing danger of
extinction. This, the loss of a national folk-art heritage, was
a universal problem in the age of urbanization and mechaniza-
tion. It had affected Spain later than most other European
countries; but it was a real danger by then, even in Andalucía,
and Falla gave much of himself to its presentation and efforts
at preservation. His association with Lorca in these enter-
prises was valuable and fruitful, and the killing of Lorca
subsequently affected him deeply.

It is no doubt a journalistic cliché to say that the Civil War
was a traumatic experience for Spain and the Spanish people;
but it is an obvious truth for all that. Probably it was bound
to come, was already inevitable well before it actually broke
out in 1936. It tore Spain apart, not only on the surface and
materially, but to the depths of her national and spiritual
being. It reflected in extreme form those widening schisms
in the national soul and psyche that have given Spain historically both her greatness and her weakness. The tragic
conflicts within Spain rose out of her history, her temperament,
her deepest spiritual sounding, her sense of destiny, her
great but too often divided existential power. Yet in the
event, in the war, the world's parasites latched onto the
Spanish agony, using it for their petty purposes, preening
their little egos or manipulating their unimportant 'causes',
knowing nothing, understanding nothing. They were not all
of that description; but too many were.

The worst thing that can happen to any society is that
it ceases to be a society and becomes a collection of conflicting

and hostile factions that do not even share a commonly accepted language or terminology to express their animosity. This is precisely what happened to Spain before and during the Civil War; and it is small wonder that after its ending, militarily, and whatever the outcome was or might have been, the texture of Spanish social, political and cultural life remained for a time fragmented and devitalized. It is also not surprising that for a considerable period a form of rigidity and introspective hamstringing of the national creative potentiality overtook the arts as well as the political organization and institutions.

Those who saw in Spanish conservatism and lack of progressive flexibility after the Civil War mere political repression and intransigence showed that they understood nothing, in specifically Spanish terms, of what that tragic conflict was really about. No doubt there was oppression and intransigence: in the circumstances it could hardly have been otherwise, however regrettable it may have appeared to the outside world. One of the worst legacies of prolonged civil conflict, and of the Spanish Civil War in particular, is a kind of lethargy, due in part to exhaustion, or excessive caution and reluctance born out of the fear of initiating another such tragedy. Even the most militant elements within Spain could have been excused for hesitating to take that risk. One may regret it, even censure it from the safety of a stable political and social environment; but it remained an inescapable fact for those who experienced it from within.

The Civil War gave Spain a re-formation of her sense of destiny, of outlying guardianship. Both sides believed they were called upon to defend the honour and dignity of civilization against the powers of darkness. If you supported the Republicans, the loyalists as they were then called, you believed they were sustaining freedom and democracy against Fascism and injustice and persecution: if you were for the Insurgents, the Nationalists, you believed with no less fervent conviction that they were holding back the advancing menace and corrupting force of international Communism cynically manipulated from Moscow. And despite excesses and atrocities on both sides, inevitable in such a context, from within Spain both beliefs were tenable and both were held with passionate conviction, leaving aside the unavoidable camp followers and hangers-on, often from the worldwide sources of political exploitation. From outside Spain it may have looked the same but was not. Most of the outside intervention in the Spanish conflict was anything but altruistic, never understood the real and meaningful motivations, never cared for the reality that was the Spanish tragedy with all its internal tensions and virtually unbearable, unbridgeable schisms in the national life and psyche. No one really supposes that the Spanish Civil War was merely, or even primarily, political

In the event it was the Nationalists under General Franco who carried the day; and Franco was destined to rule Spain for 38 years, until his death. It seemed at the time, with the world situation rapidly deteriorating and international war imminent, as though the forces of Nazi-Fascist darkness had prevailed, to the disadvantage of the democratic and civilized ideals. From the standpoint of those years the Franco victory looked ominous, both for Spain herself and for Europe as a whole. But after 1945, with the Russian colours flying free and the 'Cold War' a new fact of world politics, the picture began to take on a somewhat different aspect.

Against the more dire predictions and fears, during the course of the Hitler war Franco had, with some skill and resource and with much typical Spanish obstinacy, contrived to avoid being caught on the other prong of the devil's tail, thereby demonstrating once again that Spain's problems and struggles were and remain her own and are not to be used for anyone else's convenience. And today, with a new régime and a monarchy restored, Spain stands once again on the brink of a fresh attempt to resolve her historical dilemma of passionate duality and internal conflicting currents of spiritual and emotional opposition. It took time, as in the circumstances it was always bound to. But within the context of Spanish national evolution time is not all that important.

This is not a political book and it is not going to degenerate into political polemic. But no nation and people can pass through an experience like the Spanish Civil War without it leaving indelible marks for years afterwards, not only on the social and political structure but equally, if not more, upon the cultural epicentre. When a nation is threatened or oppressed from without, its population will unite and sink internal differences, and its creative artists will lend their voices to the inspiration of resistance; but when the conflict is internal everything becomes divisive, there is no centre of national identity, no point of clear focus. This was the fate of Spain in the 1930s, and it inevitably had a lasting effect upon her music and arts.

For Falla himself the strain was great. He lived out the Civil War in Granada, isolated, ill, unhappy. The nature of his illness is mysterious; but there seems little doubt that it was at least partly psychological. He himself attributed it to 'bad dental treatment' (Pahissa); but that seems more an excuse than a reason. Whether his immobility and personal impotence during those years was directly 'sympathetic' with Spain's agony and its consequent creative inhibition, or whether it was something deep rooted in his own sensitive psyche, or something of both, is now virtually impossible to determine. But it is beyond doubt that the pain of his country was a deep source of anguish and suffering to him.

So far as the issues of the war were concerned, Falla was simply and passionately convinced that the real, the enduring and undying Spain was Catholic Spain in all its historical splendour and its contemporary struggle. But he would not take sides openly, never allowed himself to be used as fuel for any fire, as propaganda or material for slogans. His deep Christian faith made him anti-war in any form; but he seems to have recognized, if with reluctance, that the war once started could not be stopped until the issue was settled. He was once asked for an anthem by the Nationalists; but he declined, pleading ill health: all he would offer was an arrangement of a number, 'Canto de los Almogavares', from Pedrell's opera *Los Pirineos*. It was not satisfactory, did not incite people to kill or be killed for the 'cause'. But it was as far as he would go. Well or ill he was not willing to feed passions now dangerously out of hand or provoke more violence than was abroad already. The death of his friend Garcia Lorca no doubt still tortured him and made him the more determined to keep his hands clean and his mouth shut. It was not that he didn't understand: he understood all too well.

One of the inevitable legacies of bitter and prolonged civil strife is that many on the losing side will subsequently become *émigrés*. Thus the cultural no less than the political identity of the nation will become further fragmented and divided against itself, and the process of recovering national unity correspondingly retarded. When a major part of the nation becomes actual or potential exiles, not through free choice but from a kind of enforced necessity and with little possibility of return for at least a generation, the results can be nothing but debilitating, no matter how vigorous, determined and enthusiastic the new 'loyalists' may be.

Falla himself was an exile for the latter years of his life, when he lived with his ever devoted sister in a remote part of Argentina. But there was never any suggestion that he was a political refugee. Indeed, he would have been welcomed back in Spain any time he liked to return after his departure in 1939, after the end of the Civil War.*

The immediate cause of his leaving Spain was almost accidental. He received an invitation from the Institución Cultural Española of Buenos Aires to present some concerts as part of the celebrations of its 25th anniversary. Cautious to the last, concerned with his health to the point of hypochondria, Falla at first hesitated, then consulted his doctors who advised him to go. Again, the hesitation and the ultimate decision were probably psychological. But whatever the deeper reasons, he went and he did not return. At least not in this life. After a funeral service in the cathedral of Córdoba in the Argentine, his embalmed body was taken back to Spain to be buried with honour in the crypt of Cadiz Cathedral.

The exile of Manuel de Falla was therefore voluntary and non-political. Not so in the case of many others who felt, rightly or wrongly and depending on their beliefs and their former activities, that they had no place in Franco's Spain or no wish to find a place. One such, and by far the most important from the point of view of Spanish music, was Roberto Gerhard. A Spaniard of Swiss parentage, Gerhard

*See note 7

was born in Valls in Catalonia in 1896. Like any number of middle-class youngsters, he had to overcome parental opposition to a musical career; but once he was set upon his course he soon revealed a major talent. He studied piano with Granados in Barcelona during 1915 and 1916 and was Felipe Pedrell's last pupil from 1915 to 1922. He soon began to compose, but it was not until he went to study with Schoenberg, first in Vienna and later in Berlin, that Gerhard found his true musical voice. He worked with Schoenberg and his other disciples between 1923 and 1928, with the predictable result that he joined the ranks of the serialists and followed in Schoenberg's footsteps as a starting point for his own creative maturing.

It has sometimes been claimed that Gerhard went to Schoenberg in order to break free of the impasse of the regionalism of most contemporary Spanish music. But, as I have shown, Falla had already achieved that: after Falla's mature works no Spanish composer of genuine talent needed to be bogged down in the more facile aspects of popular Spanish music. That was not Gerhard's problem. Gerhard went to Schoenberg to find himself musically, not because he was hamstrung by his national inheritance but quite simply because his particular musical faculty demanded and required that he took that direction. Many other composers of the time studied with Schoenberg and adopted Schoenberg's methods and theories, but only Gerhard appears to have been charged with having to do so to escape from a national cul-de-sac. No doubt the Schoenbergian apostleship did bend his musical course towards its proper compass point. But it did so because of its own innermost nature rather than for any reasons of escape from or avoidance of a danger that no longer existed.

Between 1928, when he completed his studies with Schoenberg, and 1938, when he left Spain following the defeat of the Republicans, Gerhard composed a certain amount of music but was not prolific. He was much occupied with administration, in his native Catalonia and then with the central government in Madrid during 1937 and 1938. Among the works of that decade were the Wind Quintet, in which he first used a serial technique (though not yet a 12-tone

one), two ballets, a cantata for soprano, baritone, chorus and orchestra, *L'Alta Naixenca en Jaune*, and a setting of *6 Catalan Folk Songs*.

After his departure from Spain Gerhard was offered, at the instigation of Edward J. Dent, a research scholarship at King's College, Cambridge. Thereafter he considered himself an English composer. And indeed, his continuing involvement in English musical life justified that claim. All the same, a man does not alter the basic constituents of his mind and temperament simply because he changes his place of residence, and Roberto Gerhard remained to the end of his days (he died in 1970) in every important respect a Spanish musician. His later music, of startling originality and sonic exuberance, is perhaps not nationally identifiable at all; yet it has a certain ingrained lucidity, directness and elegance that bespeak a Latin origin, and a toughness of intellect that is certainly in the line of Spanish music at its best (i.e. Falla), even if it is not only Spanish.

It has been argued by some that Gerhard's music is largely song-orientated in its basic structure, and that this is generally speaking an English musical characteristic. This is perfectly true in the overall sense; but it is also a characteristic of Spanish music, so it does not appear to signify very greatly, either way, even if it does point yet a further link between Spanish and English music. Certainly Gerhard, despite his apprenticeship to Schoenberg, was not a musical constructionist: he was rather a man of vivid imagination and immense creative vitality of a kind that suggests the warm south and the passions of the sun.

It is the inner nature of Gerhard's music that makes and keeps him an essentially Spanish composer more than any external characteristics. Yet those characteristics are frequently present and their incidence decisively demonstrates that the 'Spanishness' of his genius was operative at all levels, under the skin and often above it. Take the ballet *Don Quixote*, written during 1940 and 1941 and after he had settled in Cambridge. This is as 'Spanish' as anything in Falla (or Albéniz). Yet it is a serial composition, quite strict in its way, based upon a 12-tone row derived from the principal thematic material, the Don Quixote theme in 'skeleton'. Serial or not, this music is totally Spanish, both in the obvious (though it is not 'obvious' in the pejorative sense) and the deeper running manner. It is in a number of ways analagous to the earlier Falla and a little less decisive than *The Three Cornered Hat*, certainly less than *El retablo*, though the provenance of the latter is different and therefore the conjunction is only obliquely relevant.

Don Quixote is only one of Roberto Gerhard's works of a definite Spanish character to have been written after he had left Spain. He too wrote a homage to his old teacher, a symphony entitled 'Pedrelliana', or 'Homenaje a Pedrell', also based upon themes from Pedrell's opera *La Celestina*; and it is a better piece than Falla's. The list does not end there.

But the real importance of Roberto Gerhard in the story of contemporary Spanish music is not that he continued to compose in an identifiably 'Spanish' style but that he was the only Spanish composer with enough talent to follow Falla and consolidate the position won for Spanish music by Falla in the international field. If Gerhard had been able, or willing, to live on in Spain he might have inspired a further evolution of Spanish music from the vantage point of Falla's pioneering work based upon Pedrell's crusading activities, and therefore beginning from the same original base. But the Civil War put an end to that possibility.

It looks again like the jinx that historically lies upon the full emergence of Spanish music: Arriaga and Usandizaga dying mere boys and before they had time to fulfil their promise; Albéniz dying before his 50th birthday; Granados drowned as a result of war, also short of 50; Gerhard exiled by political exigency. And how many gifted musicians, known or unknown, on both sides, dead in the cauldron of the Civil War?

Gerhard's best music has a surge and vitality of the same order as Falla's. And a certain amount of its essential Spanishness resides in that; a vivacity and vitality born perhaps in the hard earth and the hard spiritual dominion of Spain and the great historic Spaniards. It is, like so much else, a quality difficult to define accurately, to analyse and elucidate, but easy enought to identify. And it is precisely this quality that is lacking in most of the Spanish composers who worked around and after Falla, in Spain or outside. Turina was a competent musician, more Germanically biased in his style than is usual for a Latin composer of his type, a useful purveyor of Spanish pictures in music. Debussy's description of Turina's best known composition is quoted by Ann Livermore:

> *La Procession del Rocio* is set out as a beautiful fresco. The frank contrasts of light and shade render listening easy in spite of the work's dimensions. Like Albéniz, J. Turina is strongly influenced by popular music and still hesitates in his development, finding it useful to make use of illustrious contemporary sources. One hopes J. Turina will pass them by and listen to more familiar voices.

And it is deadly, its bland tone from the usually sharp-tongued Debussy an obvious piece of calculated politeness aimed to kill. Maybe that is an exaggeration; but the piece itself is too bland to touch any exposed nerve or depth of reality.

Turina's *Canto a Sevilla* is better; but even it tends to meander into vague atmospherics without getting anywhere. And the popular *Danzas fantásticas* are expertly written and at least one is melodically engaging. Pleasant music, undoubtedly, all of it; music for which there is a clear and useful place. But not music of moment in any context, national or international.

And so it is with much Spanish music that followed. It is regional, parochial, agreeable, sometimes surprising, occasionally original in a small way; but virtually none of it memorable beyond its performance. In one or two cases, as with Joaquìn Rodrigo, the music and its composer seem to lie somewhere between the two, as also in their own ways do Albéniz and Granados. Rodrigo has gained international fame with his *Concierto de Aranjuez* for guitar and orchestra, and based upon that with the *Fantasía para un gentilhombre* and lesser still with the *Concierto madrigal* and *Concierto Andaluz*, all three for guitar with orchestra, the last with four guitars.

Also with some solo music for guitar. Characteristically, hardly any of Rodrigo's music away from the guitar is well known outside Spain, apart from a pleasant *Concierto-serenata* for harp and orchestra which has had a limited exposure, and one or two neat piano pieces.

Rodrigo seems the nearest Spain has produced, at least inside Spain, to a successor to Manuel de Falla. But again, although Rodrigo's music is expert, imaginative, colourful, definitely Spanish but not inhibitingly so, it tends to lack that essential force of inner vitalism that apparently only Falla and Roberto Gerhard could command; and its *evocación*, though strong, is a little too diffused. There is perhaps, here and with others, not enough true *duende*.

All the same, Rodrigo does stand out as a genuine, gifted Spanish composer whose work is capable of interesting an international audience not only for its local colour and obvious 'Spanishness'.

That passionate vitality: it is the key to the larger question. It is the vitality of on the one hand the mystical visions of Victoria, on the other of the dark soundings of flamenco and *cante jondo*. It is the endemic force and revelation of the totality of the Spanish soul and character. It is not only physical but also emotional, and then the Spaniards call it *duende*. Without it Spanish music is but a pale and ineffectual imitation; though written by Spaniards and performed by Spaniards no less, if it has not this passion and vitality it is not genuine and must be placed on the level of the merely picturesque and the far-ranging ephemeral.

That the central importance of Falla in the resurgence and continuation of Spanish music was recognized by the younger composers is demonstrated by the formation, immediately after Falla's death, of the Círculo Manuel de Falla with the honourable intention and objective of maintaining through the difficult years following the conclusion of the Spanish Civil War and then emphasized by the impact of the Second World War, certain social and artistic ideals with something of Falla's own integrity and uncompromising firmness of purpose. It was a gesture on the right side; but unfortunately it lacked the one ingredient necessary to give it creative teeth

—a composer sufficiently gifted to take on the élite mantle of Falla as a composer. It was in any case a tall order; but then all orders worth taking notice of are tall and if they are not taller than any present expect or suppose then they are not in the lineage of what has inspired the effort in the first place.

Of the older composers working in Spain after the Civil War, talent was reasonably current, as might be expected in any one place and any one time; but genius was elusive. Joaquin Nin Culmell, though he worked mostly in California; Federico Mompou whose piano music has a distinction of a relatively small if marked scale; Xavier Montsalvatge, composer of songs and other small genre pieces; these and others ran and run the competence of Spanish music. But for a larger and more comprehensive figure it has yet to wait.

And it is important. Though a certain vein of current criticism asserts that the general democratic level is what matters, and the 'great man' is outmoded—Stockhausen and Cornelius Cardew propagate this view—in art it is a fallacy and only the major figure (as Stockhausen himself is) can set the pace and establish that depth of new vision and breadth of new perception upon which the average talent (if there is such a thing) can build and be nourished. The Stockhausen-Cardew view may have some relevance where the musical tradition is deeply entrenched, the musical current strong and irresistible; but where it is not and has still to be cherished and encouraged, the example of a central powerful figure is essential, if only to reveal what can be done with existing materials, as Falla himself did and had to do; as Bartók did in Hungary and Sibelius in Finland. Without these the potentiality of their nations' indigenous music might never have fully emerged.

English music of its own period of renaissance was more fortunate. After the 'big name' pioneers—Elgar, Vaughan Williams, Bax if you will, Holst—there was a following generation—Walton, Tippett, Britten—of equal stature to lead across to the new set, the progressives as they may be called, not quite accurately, the experimentalists or even those of the avant-garde, though that must as a term be taken with caution and is best avoided as a label. But in Spain there was no such continuation, in quality rather than quantity. After Falla? . . .

Gerhard was in exile, and in any case his music is curiously not highly regarded in Spain; even more curiously it is seen as not genuinely vital and full-blooded. How much of that criticism is directed less at the music itself than conditioned, albeit unconsciously, by a political motivation is always hard to say; and in a country like Spain with its recent tragic history virtually impossibly so, and maybe even for the Spaniards themselves.

One thing Spanish music is not is excessively theoretical; and this it shares with nearly all the Latin countries, certainly with France and Italy. That is not to say that it is deficient in brainwork: Falla's technique of natural resonance was worked out from a theory. But the profoundly theoretical, the deeply metaphysical, the protestingly methodical belongs to the Austro-German tradition, to the Wagner-Schoenberg line and succession. That in itself is of no lasting moment; it is a fact not only of music, not only of art in any form, but of the whole of life.

As a general rule, when a Spanish musician takes it into his head to traffic in too much theory, it tends to sound as though it has strayed in on a passing wind. Curiously (but perhaps not so curiously in view of his Swiss parentage) Roberto Gerhard, though he objected to complicated analytical expositions and believed, as Beethoven did and as all intelligent persons do, and certainly as Schoenberg did, that what is important is that the music should be heard as an experience first of all and that the means by which the work is done is the composer's business alone, was inclined to annotate in oddly pedantic and formalized phrases. At times one might almost be reading Schoenberg translated. Such phrases as 'a high rate of eventuation' and the like come out of no English (or Spanish) lexicon—though they may come out of an American one—and occasionally when reading Gerhard one has the impression of a theoretician on the loose. Erik Satie once said: 'Monsieur Ravel has refused the Légion d'Honneur but all his music accepts it'. In a similar line it could be said that Roberto Gerhard often sounded the theoretical note but all his music rejected it. In any case, though, Gerhard was a wit and a raconteur. And he was Spanish in words as well as music: 'Performance is the "moment of truth" '.

Despite the lack of enthusiasm on the part of Spanish critics, it seems undeniable that the loss through political exile of Roberto Gerhard was hardly less a disaster for Spanish music than the torpedoing of Granados in 1916. Though Gerhard, unlike Granados, was able to continue composing, his influence on the music of Spain was minimal. Indeed, his great period of original creativity came in the later years of his life and was an amazing event or happening; as astonishing in its way as Verdi's last burst of creative power, longer lasting and more prolific than Verdi's though instigated at a lesser age. The analogy is only half valid; but these sudden spurts and twists of genius never cease to astonish; or if they do they shouldn't, for once genius ceases to surprise it fundamentally ceases to function at full force and potency.

The current Spanish music scene is busy and appears encouraging; but it is not yet out of the wood. The double hiatus of first a lack of any central stabilizing figure after Falla and a failure of close contact with the musical world at large, due initially to the Civil War and subsequently to isolation during the Second World War, and then to the exile of many who might and would in other circumstances have formed a firm core, still operates. I have spoken of Roberto Gerhard; but there are others.

The Falla tradition could have been, and in a certain sense was, carried on by two of Falla's favourite pupils, the brothers Ernesto and Rodolfo Halffter. Ernesto's *Concierto para Guitarra y Orquesta* is an interesting and skilfully written piece that might well be taken up by the guitar virtuosi (it has been by Narcisso Yepes) as an alternative to endless repetitions of Rodrigo's *Aranjuez*. It is a generically 'Spanish' work with echoes of 'middle' Falla in places plus an overall feel that owes to the example of the master. It generally avoids what Constant Lambert wickedly but accurately called 'the monotonous *espieglerie* of the cabaret dancer' which all too often served to overlay the true musical voice of Spain and against which successive Spanish composers since Pedrell struggled. But as with so many post-Falla Spanish works it lacks those internal tensions in the melodic line and the digging in of the associated rhythm and harmony even in quiet and reflective music which gives vitality and depth to Falla's own music and defines its particularly Spanish quality. Rodrigo's *Concierto de Aranjuez,* especially in its fine slow movement, has this inner tension, which no doubt accounts for its enduring popularity both with players and with the public, even to the point of having that slow movement adapted, with reasonable success, by top ranking jazz musicians like Miles Davis and the Modern Jazz Quartet. No doubt for some that will be a doubtful distinction; but the results do tend to confirm the music's strength and indestructibility.

But Ernesto Halffter, who followed his master's example in the ballet theatre with considerable accomplishment, has lived most of his later life in Portugal; and his brother became an exile in Mexico after Franco's victory, so that neither has played a full part in the re-emergence of Spanish music following the national disruption caused by the Civil War, even though Ernesto performed a major service in 'completing' and editing *Atlántida* and continued it with his activities as a conductor.

By no means all the 'middle generation' composers left Spain after the Republican defeat in 1938. One whose work did much to restore the situation was the Catalan composer and conductor, the late Eduardo Toldrá. Toldrá's gifts were many and various, and he might well have achieved more as a composer if he had not devoted so much of his time to teaching, conducting and general musical administration, notably in his native Catalonia. He became one of the most internationally acclaimed of Spanish conductors: in the late 1950s he made a recording of *The Three Cornered Hat* with the French National Radio Orchestra that for vividness of re-creation has not been surpassed (the delineation of the corregidor by the French bassoonist is so full of humour and character that it deserves an Oscar on its own).

He also conducted the first concert performance of *Atlántida* at the Teatro del Liceo in Barcelona, where he directed the regular opera season for many years, in 1961. As Ann Livermore rightly says: 'His selfless dedication to these musical causes was exceptional, and has left both public taste and musical organization immeasurably improved'.

All these composers, plus others, some of them younger and the creators of the Círculo Manuel de Falla, worked in what may loosely be called the Falla tradition; that is, they followed Falla in striving to perpetuate a Spanish music with an international European style, whether like Rodrigo and Toldrá they stayed in Spain, or like the Halffters they became expatriates. There were of course many variants due to personal identity and regional diversity; but overall the ideals and achievements of Falla continued to dominate.

This, however, continued an already established tradition. In the world outside Spain other and more 'advanced' or 'progressive' (both bad words, but they will have to do) ideas and ideals were activating the musical world. And although, partly due to the double hiatus and partly because of innate Spanish conservatism reinforced by the rigidities of the post-Civil War period, these new ideas came late to Spain, they percolated through in time into the Spanish musical bloodstream. A new generation of Spanish composers came to the fore taking their cue not from what had already been achieved, principally by Falla (though at their best embracing the deeper implications of that also) as from the wider currents of European modernism. In one sense, this new generation reversed the earlier process: whereas Falla and his colleagues and immediate successors had striven to create and inject into the European mainstream an international style based upon Spanish national and historical idioms, the new men sought to infuse Spanish music as it had so far emerged with the ideas of the main European and American protagonists, beginning with Schoenberg, though in this case long after Gerhard had given the lead, and proceeding from there to Varèse, Stockhausen, Boulez, Cage and the post-Webern serialists. Thus the concept of 'musica española con vistas a Europa' which had inspired Falla and originated with Pedrell, took on a different if complementary meaning. But it still retained in its new form as laid down in the manifesto *Música abierta*, its original intention and ambition, to make Spanish music a true and significant contribution to the European totality.

The oldest member of the 'new set' in Spain was Joaquín Homs. Homs was born in 1906 and so belongs in age to an earlier generation; but his musical sympathies lay squarely in the Schoenberg camp. Most of them, however, were younger men born in the decade and a half or so after the First World War, and one of them, Cristóbal Halffter, carried an honoured name from the immediate past into the challenging future. A nephew of Ernesto and Rodolfo Halffter, he was born in Madrid in 1930 and studied first with Conrado del Campo, a Spanish composer who died in 1953 and like Turina showed musical sympathies with German rather than Latin musical traditions, especially with Richard Strauss's orchestral style, and later with Alexander Tansman. After winning the National Music Award in 1953, he became professor of composition and conductor at the Madrid Conservatoire. A prolific and unusually gifted composer, Cristóbal Halffter exploits an extended serial technique, making some use of electronic devices. His *Espejos* for four percussionists and multiple tape shows the influence of Edgard Varèse. The tape here is used not to produce direct electronic effects but to enable the sections of the music to be played simultaneously. But Halffter has always followed a course of his own, seeking forms and techniques that exactly complement his own positive and decided ideas. His ballet *Saeta* and a number of vocal compositions show the essentially Spanish cast of his mind and faculty, though he is hardly a 'nationalist' in the older, Falla-based sense, even though the texture of his musical thinking is underlined by his nationality in an unspecific way.

The Basques have always made a strong contribution to Spanish art and culture; and Luis de Pablo carries that sturdy tradition into the modern age. Like several of these composers, and others not Spanish, Pablo began in a more or less traditional manner, then switched around 1959 to a full-blooded 'progressive' and experimental style. He too was born in 1930, in Bilbao, though he studied in Madrid. He was always involved in various avant-garde movements and founded two groups for the performance of Spanish and other contemporary music.

Post-Webern serialism is notable in the work of Carmelo Bernaola who was born in 1929 and studied with Julio Gómez at the Madrid Conservatoire and, after winning the Premo de Roma in 1959, with Petrassi, Tansman and Maderna. As well as a Webern-like use of seriality and associated textures, Bernaola sometimes combines it with a variant of Bartók's 'arch' form. The results can be impressive.

Another who broke with his own musical past early on in favour of the 'new music' experiments was José Maria Mestress-Quadreny, born in Barcelona in 1929. He has been strongly influenced by abstract painting, and it shows in his music, for it frequently appears to follow the same linear patterns. He is one of those, by no means uncommon nowadays, who invites the performers to take an active part in the presentation and interpretation of his scores, sometimes to the point of directly contributing to the act of creation. So also does Juan Hidalgo, who was born in 1927 and has been active in adapting some of John Cage's ideas to the Spanish musical idiom. His settings of Góngora could be thought to give him a small link with Falla; but that, though valid, is incidental. The real importance of it lies in the way Spanish texts tend to bring out the essential nationality of these modern Spanish composers in a way their instrumental music sometimes does not. Maybe this is more or less irrelevant in the contemporary context, when in any case artistic nationalism is *démodé*, often regarded as the faded relic of a romantic and romaticized past. But that is not to be taken as the final, irrevocable truth either.

The importance of language in this context is that it helps to obviate the danger of artistic anonymity. One of the perils of adopting a consciously (or self-consciously) 'contemporary' style, whether it is serial, post-serial, aleatoric or whatever else, is that unless the composer has a strongly ingrained creative personality it is all too easy to become merely anonymous; as easy, and as fatal, as it is to sound suddenly 'old fashioned'. It is as easy to write nondescript serial or post-serial music today as it was to produce (by the metre) non-descript, anonymous sonata form music in the eighteenth century. And it is a danger by no means always avoided by some of these Spanish composers. A music-publisher friend of mine after listening to some of these Spanish composi-tions, once retorted with some disdain: 'Spanish music? It might just as well have been written in a Berlin sewer.'

The judgement was harsh; but it was not entirely unmerited. Perhaps the desire to 'Europeanize' Spanish music tends to go too far at times. It was all very well for Stravinsky to cosmopolitanize Russian music; but Stravinsky's creative personality was so decisive and so tough that it could get away with virtually anything. For lesser beings it is necessary to tread more warily; to keep one foot at least fairly securely anchored on the home base.

In the end, of course, it is all part of what Stephen Spender once described as 'the struggle of the modern'.

There is as yet no Spanish Boulez, or Berio, or Stockhausen, or Cage. Perhaps that in itself is neither remarkable nor astonishing. And maybe it is asking too much in any case, keeping in mind the various disasters and consequent inhibi-tions that have afflicted the Spanish nation in this century. But not only that: major figures do not appear for the asking, and are never to be taken for granted. All the same, the dangers of creative anonymity, even in a country with as positive a national identity as Spain, are ever present. Unless the centre is held firm there is always liable to be a diffusion, if not an actual dispersion, of what talent there is. That is why the setting of native texts tends to focus the creative image and define the deeper provenance. A language, any language, has a sound, a texture, a particular dynamic and inflexion of its own, a specific resonance in phrase and sentence, often in single words, that leads the composer, if he is a true artist, to match it in his music, whatever his idiom and tech-nique may chance to be, 'traditional' or 'modern'. It is not of course, a sure safefall, a certain panacea: it is perfectly possible to write anonymous vocal music; hardly less of a problem than to deliver anonymous instrumental or orchestral music. But the exigencies of language do lay a particular charge on a composer, and, if he knows his business, will assist him to avoid the trap of the anonymous and the creatively nondescript. And it will assist him indirectly as well as directly; for if he attends to the essential nature and character of his language it will help to vitalize and give distinction to his non-vocal melodic and rhythmic invention as well as his overtly linguistic production. This is a universal principle: it was as true for Brahms as for Bartók or Janáček—or Falla. It may not, indeed in advanced and experimental music it will not, lie upon or even near the surface. But it will still be operative at some level.

A complete and detailed examination of the contemporary developments of Spanish music, or music in general, is not within the intended scope of this book. It is concerned primarily with the renaissance of Spanish music instigated by Felipe Pedrell and brought to initial fruition by Manuel de Falla. All the same, the first thing that is necessary, if a national creative force in any of the arts, indeed in any area of the national life is to prosper, is a high degree of productivity. Without that, at any time, it is unlikely that the full and true voice will emerge and remain continuously potent. It was within an upsurge of productivity that Falla's own genius grew and matured. And although his own production was limited, it was of such a quality and of such vitality that it released national energies and potentialities far beyond its actual sphere of activity. In the contemporary history of Spanish music Manuel de Falla remains the pivot and focal point without which much that has been achieved since his life and death might have been seriously withheld, at least damagingly diluted. That is not too strong an assessment, too fanciful an exaggeration. That there has been no one of his stature since is both an observable fact and a commentary on the particular circumstances of the Spanish nation since the high tide of his own career. And perhaps those circumstances themselves had a significant bearing on his inability to finish his own *Atlántida* and make it, as it was always intended to be, his masterpiece, the testament of his entire life and work, and in a particular sense the testament of modern Spanish music.

But that was not to be; just as many things in and for Spain were not to be. There is strong evidence to believe that, after the years of trial and suffering and then further years of retrenchment in the wake of that trial and that suffering, the Spanish nation and people stand now upon the threshold of a new resurgence, a culmination of the rising from the ashes, a period of recovered greatness that has always been inherent but for too many centuries after her Golden Century has been for one reason and another frustrated and too often aborted.

And there is no less evidence to believe that the musical renaissance initiated by Pedrell and consolidated by Falla, is also gathering new force. The question that remains in the mind as far as that is concerned is: How far would the course of Spanish music after Falla's last works have been encouraged and vitalized had not Roberto Gerhard, the one Spanish composer of genius in line with Falla's own, despite what certain Spanish critics assert to the contrary, not felt obliged to leave Spain and spend the rest of his life an exile in England, a self-proclaimed English composer? Spanish music's loss was no doubt English music's gain; but it remains a large, if unanswerable, question for all that.

One other thing, which is not a question but a certainty: Spain is a profoundly musical nation and has a profoundly musical culture. The depth and strength of the Spanish musical heritage is conclusively demonstrated by what Manuel de Falla was able to do with it in contemporary terms, and the way in which, although it has by no means always been recognized, he did not close the door but left it open for his successors to pass through. Factors other than the purely musical worked to obscure that truth and to keep the door swinging on its hinges rather than clearly open and immediately usable.

Spanish indigenous music is easy enough to imitate on the surface, probably the easiest of all to parody, as Lord Berners for one wittily demonstrated, thereby leading as sharp-witted and penetrating a critic as Constant Lambert down a false trail. But it is a basic law of parody that only that which is itself of inherent quality can lead to parodies of quality. If you parody rubbish, you make rubbish. You can parody late Henry James, or Hemingway, and you will achieve something worth the trouble (Hemingway sometimes parodied himself, but that is not quite the same thing). But if you parody slick journalese you will only get more slick journalese. The ability both to provoke and to withstand good parody is in itself part of the inherent strength and integrity of the original.

It was Manuel de Falla more than any other who in our time revealed and exposed the truth of that, along with much else. He was the creative embodiment of both historical and modern Spain's mind and soul. And by one of those strange paradoxes which seem to belong uniquely to Spain, his own creative frustrations were perhaps also the embodiment of his country's frustrations and misadventures.

Falla's music is, as he intended it should be, strove valiantly to make it, universal. Yes, it is universal; but like Cervantes, like *Don Quixote* itself, the quintessential Spanish book as *The Pilgrim's Progress* is the quintessential English book, it is first of all, primarily and most profoundly about Spain.

APPENDICES

THE COMPOSITIONS OF
MANUEL DE FALLA

(a) PUBLISHED WORKS:

La vida breve (1904–05). Opera in two Acts and four Scenes. Libretto by Carlos Fernández Shaw. (Published by Max Eschig, Paris, 1913).

Pièces espagnoles (Cuatro piezas españolas) (1906). For piano. (Published by Duraud et Cie, Paris, 1909).

Trois mélodies—(Les Colombes; Chinoiserie; Séguidille)—(1906). Words by Théophile Gautier. For voice and piano. (Published by Rouart, Lerolle et Cie, Paris, 1910).

Siete canciones populares españolas (Seven Popular Spanish Songs) —(El paño moruna; Seguidilla murciana; Asturiana; Jota; Nana; Canción; Polo)—(1914). For voice and piano. (Published by Max Eschig, Paris, 1922).

El amor brujo (1914–15). Ballet with songs in one Act. Scenario by G. Martínez Sierra.

Noches en los jardines de España (Nights in the Gardens of Spain) (1911–15). Symphonic impressions for piano and orchestra (En el Generalife; Danza lejana; En los jardines de la Sierra de Córdoba).

El sombrero de tres picos (The Three Cornered Hat—Le Tricorne) (1916–19). Ballet in two Scenes. Scenario by G. Martínez Sierra, after Alarcón.

Fantasía baetica (or *bética*) (1919). For piano.

Homenaje ('Le Tombeau de Claude Debussy') (1920). For guitar.

El retablo de Maese Pedro (Master Peter's Puppet Show) (1919–22). Puppet opera for voices and orchestra. Libretto by Falla, based on an episode from *Don Quixote* by Miguel de Cervantes.

Psyché (1924). For voice, flute, harp, violin, viola, and violoncelle. Words by Georges Jean-Aubry.

Concerto per clavicembalo (1923–26). For harpsichord (or piano), flute, oboe, clarinet, violin and violoncello.

Soneto a Córdoba (1927). For voice and harp. Words by Luis de Góngora.

Balada de Mallorca (1933). For mixed *a cappella* choir. Words by Jacinto Verdaguer.

Pour le tombeau de Paul Dukas (1935). For piano.

Homenajes (1920–38). For orchestra (Fanfare sobre el nombre de E. F. Arbós; a Cl. Debussy (Elegia de la guitarra); a Paul Dukas (Spes vitae); Pedrilliana).

Atlántida (1927–46—unfinished). Scenic cantata in a Prologue and three Acts. Text adapted by Falla from the Catalan by Jacinto Verdaguer. (Revised, edited and completed by Ernesto Halffter, 1961; final revised and shortened version, 1976.)

Note: The 1976 'final version' has now been recorded by EMI (HMV (SQ) SLS5116: Am. Angel SBLX3852), by Spanish forces under Rafael Fruhbeck de Burgos. The opportunity given by this admirable enterprise to study *Atlántida* in performance ('the moment of truth') confirms generally the original impression that, although there is much really fine music, altogether worthy of its composer, the whole does not achieve true stylistic unity, or a total synthesis leading to an unimpeachable universal style based upon the totality of Spanish musical idioms that its creator originally envisaged. It is thus not the ultimate, and triumphant, vindication of all that Falla had worked and had striven for throughout his life. It is impressive, and in parts more than that; but the sense of final consummation is missing. It does not displace the Concerto for Harpsichord as Falla's most conclusive word on Spanish music in the contemporary world. If he had lived to complete *Atlántida* himself it might, and on the eivdence would, have been a different story. But that is another of the great 'ifs'; and it does not in any way detract from the value of Ernesto Halffter's long and devoted labours.

The booklet accompanying this set contains not only the libretto and commentaries on the work, but also a number of extracts from the correspondence between Falla and

José María Sert which persisted over many years, until the latter's death.

The above list comprises all the works Falla himself wished to acknowledge, and are issued as his complete catalogue by his principal publishers J. & W. Chester/Edition Wilhelm Hansen London Ltd (the 1961 edition of *Atlántida* was published by Ricordi). But there are some earlier pieces not sanctioned by Falla for publication as part of his official *oeuvre* but which found their way into circulation. These include three piano pieces—*Vals-Capricho*; *Serenata Andaluza*; *Nocturno*—which he wrote in his youth and which are collected together for convenience. They have been recorded by Joaquin Achúcarro in a recital which also includes the *Fantasía baetica* and the *Cuatro piezas* entitled 'Homage to Manuel de Falla' and was issued in honour of his centenary in 1976 (RCA TRLI 7073). Achúcarro gives the date as 1890, but Ronald Crichton puts them as *c*.1900–1902. They were apparently published in Falla's youth, in Madrid, without copyright. They were later issued in America without Falla's permission and finally, by the Union Musical Española, Madrid, in 1940. They are pleasant little pieces, not particularly characteristic. There is a fourth which is usually lumped with them, a song for voice and piano, *Tus ojillos negros* to words by Cristóbal de Castro.

There is also the only *zarzuela* by Falla to have achieved publication, *Los amores de la Inés*. It came out, also from Union Musical Españolas, in 1965.

(b) UNPUBLISHED WORKS:

Fuego fatuo (Firefly). Suite for orchestra arranged by Antoni Ros Marbá and performed by him at the Granada Festival in 1976. Based on a comic opera by G. Martínez Sierra with music by Falla based on Chopin.

Limosna de Amor; *El Corneta de Ordenes*; *La Cruz de Malta*; *Las Casa de Tócame Roque*. These are the other four *zarzuelas* Falla composed in his youth. *El Corneta* and *La Cruz* were written in collaboration with Amadeo Vives, and *Limosna* had a libretto by Jackson Veyan. *La Casa*, the only one of Falla's *zarzuelas* to which he attached any importance contains an item of material which later went into the making of the Corregidor's Dance in *The Three Cornered Hat*.

As well as the above Falla did a certain amount of musical journeywork which did not, nor was intended to achieve the dignity of publication. This includes some incidental music to a Catalan performance of Shakespeare's *Othello* given by G. Martínez Sierra in Barcelona (1915); some music for classical Spanish dramas by Calderón and Lope de Vega during the 1920s, and a revision of Rossini's overture to *The Barber of Seville*. In addition, he wrote during the 1930s his own versions or arrangements of choral music from the Golden Age of Victoria, Morales, Juan del Encina, Francisco and others.

There are also a few instrumental and vocal pieces either from his extreme youth or written for some occasional purpose, none of them published, many of them lost. For full details see Ronald Crichton's *Descriptive Catalogue*. None of them bear either way on Falla's standing as a creative artist or affect his ideals of fashioning a universal Spanish musical language and idiom, though one or two may hint at things to come.

BIBLIOGRAPHY

A certain amount has been written about Falla over the years; as much perhaps as might be expected in view of his small output, but not nearly as much as his significance as an artist, both in respect to Spanish music itself and in the totality of the European music of his time, would indicate. His centenary in 1976 provoked some interest, but it did not bring forth a major study, an exhaustive biography, or a comprehensive revaluation. Obviously, a good deal has been written about him in Spain, but only some of it has been translated. The following selection covers the worthwhile books readily accessible to the English or American reader. Those with the gift of reading Spanish will find further sources in libraries or direct from Madrid. Those volumes quoted or drawn upon in the text are marked with an asterisk (*) both for reference and as further acknowledgment to their authors and publishers.

(a) BOOKS ON FALLA AND RELATED MUSICAL SUBJECTS:

ABRAHAM, GERALD, *A Hundred years of Music* (Duckworth, London, 1938, 3rd ed., 1964; also Methuen paperback, 1964). An admirable and lucid résumé of European music from the death of Beethoven, expanded to bring it up to 1963. Full of perceptive comments and analyses; sharp insights into musical nationalism in all its forms, including the Spanish variety.

CHASE, GILBERT, *The Music of Spain* (New York, 1941, 1959). This, and Trend (q.v.), are the two classic books on the subject in English. Though by no means new they contain much still valid and valuable material. Chase's book deals briefly, besides Falla, with the other Spanish composers of the period, notably Albéniz and Granados.

COLLET, HENRI, *Albéniz et Granados* (Paris, 1926).

*CRICHTON, RONALD, *Manuel de Falla : Descriptive catalogue of his works* (J. & W. Chester, London, 1976). This invaluable book gives all relevant information about Falla's composition —dates, first performances, forces involved, origins, histories; everything you need to know. It is a book primarily of facts, therefore it does not indulge in criticism, although inevitably some critical comment is included in the descriptive sections. There is also a brief biographical note. A book no student of Falla can possibly be without.

DEMARQUEZ, SUZANNE, *Manuel de Falla* (Paris, 1963; Eng. ver., New York & Canada, 1968).

FALLA, MANUEL DE, *Escritos sobre musica y musicos* (Madrid, 1950, rev. ed., 1972. English version, *Musical Writings* (Marion Boyars, London, 1978—trans. John Thomson and David Urman). Obviously essential reading: Falla was articulate, if reticent; he had strong views on music and musicians; here too is an important piece on *cante jondo*, as probing as Lorca's lecture on *duende*, and related.

*LAMBERT, CONSTANT, *Music ho!* (Faber & Faber, 1933, 1936; Faber Paperbacks, 1974). Too many general books on music, whether devoted to modern music or not, specifically, tend to pass Falla, and indeed Spanish music as a whole, off in a few lines. Apart from Gerald Abraham, their authors have nothing of interest to say on the subject. Writers as stimulating and perceptive as Wilfrid Mellers, Christopher Headington and Harold Schoenberg come into this category. Constant Lambert does not entirely qualify. Lambert had plenty to say; but he got most of it wrong, as I have argued in the text. Yet *Music ho!* is still so penetrating and pertinent on the period, so full of wit and insight, uncomfortable though some of it may be, that it remains a book to be read after more than 40 years. If only for the style, one might say—yet not only for the style.

*LIVERMORE, ANN, *A Short History of Spanish Music* (Duckworth, London, 1972). A thorough examination of the evolution and nature of Spanish music from ancient times to the present, all presented with concision and authority. Valuable in all its aspects.

OROZCO, MANUEL, *Falla* (Barcelona, 1968—illus., biog.)

*Pahissa, Jaime, *Manuel de Falla: His Life and Works* (Museum Press, London, 1954: trans. Jean Wagstaff). Later and expanded edition, Buenos Aires: *Vida y obra de Manuel de Falla.* Useful and informative, if somewhat quirky in places. The source of much personal information about Falla, with useful comments on the music by a fellow composer. Pahissa was a close personal friend of Falla in the Argentine, and as a consequence reveals many telling details from the inside. There is a Foreword by Salvador de Madariaga.

Roland, Manuel, *Manuel de Falla* (Paris, 1930).

Sopeña, Federico, *Atlántida: Introducción a Manuel de Falla* (Madrid, 1962). Father Sopeña is Madrid's leading critic and musical administrator. He approaches Falla from the deeply Christian viewpoint of Falla himself. The results are illuminating. He has also written studies of Turina and Rodrigo, also valuable. In addition he has edited and annotated Falla's writings on music.

Trend, J. B., *Manuel de Falla and Spanish Music* (New York, 1929, 1935).

(b) GENERAL BOOKS ON SPAIN:

Since Falla was so deepdyed and quintessentially a Spanish composer, and since Spain is a country that has attracted a lot of discussion and writing but a good deal less understanding, in order to help see Falla and his musical compatriots in perspective, some extra-musical reading may be useful. The following short list is recommended for that purpose.

Bertrand, Louis and Petrie, Sir Charles, *The History of Spain*, 711–1931 (Eyre and Spottiswoode, London, 1934). A brilliant, if at times controversial, compact history of Spain. Continually stimulating and authoritative. The best 'introduction' to a large subject.

Castillo-Puche, José Luis, *Hemingway in Spain* (Doubleday, New York, 1974; New English Library, London, 1975— trans. Helen R. Lane). This came out in Spain as *Hemingway: Entre la Vida y la Muerte,* a far more evocative title as well as a far more indigenously Spanish one. The well-known Spanish novelist who was Hemingway's friend over many years, gently takes Ernesto apart and puts him together again in a sometimes surprising form. But it goes deep; above all it says a huge amount about Spain and the modern Spanish life and society.

ELLIS, HAVELOCK, *The Soul of Spain* (Constable, London, 1907, 1937). The best of the older books on Spain. Though Ellis wrote a new Preface for the third edition, in 1937, when the Spanish Civil War was already half way through its course, the text dates from the decade before the First World War. It thus presents a view of Spain before the structure of its society had begun to break apart. It concerns the older, eternal, historic Spain, and in that it strikes to the heart of the matter. There is Borrow (*The Bible in Spain*) and there is Ford (*Handbook for Travellers in Spain* and *Gatherings from Spain*), the two classics in English from the nineteenth century, and both are worth reading or re-reading. But Havelock Ellis's small volume is the one to recommend from today's perspectives.

HEMINGWAY, ERNEST, *Death in the Afternoon* (London & New York, 1933 on). You have to come to it sooner or later if you love and want to understand Spain. So you may as well take it straight away. Despite some triteness, some facetious cleverness, this remains the classic exposition. Many disagree; but it will not be put down. If you can't take it, you probably can't take Spain. Hemingway the novelist of course devoted many pages to Spain. *For Whom the Bell Tolls* has not worn well; but *The Sun Also Rises* has. So have many of the short stories. The way it really was is revealed in *Hemingway in Spain*, see CASTILLO-PUCHE.

MICHENER, JAMES, *Iberia: Spanish Travels and Reflections* (Random House, New York, 1968; Secker & Warburg, London). But it is never easy. Here is a huge, rambling, discursive book so heavy you get armache trying to hold it up. But—and this is what signifies and rewards patience—Michener is a novelist (*Hawaii, Caravans, The Source*) with the novelist's eye for telling detail and the underlying pattern. The book is full of everything that can be got out of Spain, on the travelling level anyway. It doesn't prove as deep as James Morris (q.v.), not all the time. But it fills a big canvas and offers rich entertainment and a good deal of worthwhile information. It is also peppered with many photographs by the gifted Robert Vavra, dozens of them full page, the majority of real quality, an essential commentary on the text.

MORRIS, JAMES, *The Presence of Spain* (Faber & Faber, London, 1964; Harcourt Brace and World Inc., 1964: as *Spain*, Faber Paper Editions, 1970). 'Perhaps the best general book ever written on Spain,' Gerald Brenan, himself a writer on that subject called it. A tall order; but not an outrageous one. This indeed is a little book of immense worth, a short penetration. Maybe if you want to know about Spain, real Spain, this is the easy way in—easy because it is short and superbly to the point.

SEGOVIA, ANDRÉS, *An Autobiography of the Years 1893–1920* (Macmillan Publishing Co. Inc., New York, 1976; Marion Boyars, London, 1977—trans. W. F. O'Brien). Whether this should go into the musical or the general section may be a neat question. But it must go somewhere. It tells the story of one great Spaniard and his quality lies not only in his art, supreme though that has been, but also in himself; but not only of that. It has the texture, unforced, unostentatious, but firm and unmistakable, of what is best, most enduring, most typical in Spain, with a run of humour not always to be heard and a wisdom of years illuminating the turbulences of youth. Charm: but a hard indestructable centre.

SITWELL, SACHEVERELL, *Spain* (Batsford, London, 1950, rev. 1975). A modern classic; written and observed with the poet's eye and style, its reputation deservedly high.

Since the fact rather than the events of the Civil War is what pressed upon Manuel de Falla and the Spanish arts and music in general, I have included no volume devoted to that sad subject. But if one is required, for reference or to fill out a total understanding, then that by Hugh Thomas is most readily to be commended.

NOTES

1. p. 56: Thomas Rajna has recorded all Granados's piano music, much of it unfamiliar, on seven CRD LPs.

2. p. 66: Falla's specific reason for objecting to the term 'picturesque' was that he considered it more applicable to painting than to music. This makes sense; but it doesn't go the whole way. 'Picturesque' as applied to music suggests the purely colourful and descriptive—which makes it quite unsuitable for virtually all Falla's music.

3. p. 96: *A Short History of Spanish Music* (London, 1972). See Appendix II.

4. p. 104: *Job* also uses the old Renaissance dances—Galliard, Pavane, Sarabande.

5. p. 116: The physical dimensions of *Atlántida* do not invalidate the argument. It is the internal aesthetic that signifies.

6. p. 121: In this as in some other respects *Atlántida* might be seen as the Spanish counterpart of Vaughan Williams's *The Pilgrim's Progress*. Despite the failure of the original theatre production at Covent Garden, Vaughan Williams continued to insist that *The Pilgrim's Progress* was a stage work, not one for a cathedral or concert hall. Michael Kennedy has perceptively described it as a series of *tableaux vivants*. Though very different in conception, both works have a deeply religious centre. Vaughan Williams himself wrote in a letter to a friend: 'What are the great Church ceremonies but a sublimation of the dance?'; and Gustav Holst's great *Hymn of Jesus*

contains the words: 'Divine grace is dancing, ye who dance not know not what we are knowing'. Surely that would have found an echo in Falla.

7.   p. 138: For the last part of his final journey home, Falla's body was conveyed on a Spanish warship. He could, as we have seen, had he so wished, have returned to Spain at any time during his last years. There was plenty of trans-Atlantic traffic during the Second World War, especially in neutral ships. But also perhaps the fate of Granados in 1916 discouraged Spanish composers from undertaking maritime voyages in wartime.

INDEX